CULTURE SMART!
SCOTLAND

John H. Scotney

WITHDRAWN

·K·U·P·E·R·A·R·D·

First published in Great Britain 2010
by Kuperard, an imprint of Bravo Ltd
59 Hutton Grove, London N12 8DS
Tel: +44 (0) 20 8446 2440   Fax: +44 (0) 20 8446 2441
www.culturesmartguides.com
Inquiries: sales@kuperard.co.uk

Culture Smart! ® is a registered trademark of Bravo Ltd

Distributed in the United States and Canada
by Random House Distribution Services
1745 Broadway, New York, NY 10019
Tel: +1 (212) 572-2844   Fax: +1 (212) 572-4961
Inquiries: csorders@randomhouse.com

Series Editor Geoffrey Chesler
Design Bobby Birchall

ISBN 978 1 85733 492 0

British Library Cataloguing in Publication Data
A CIP catalogue entry for this book is available from the
British Library

Printed in Malaysia

This book is available for special discounts for bulk purchases
for sales promotions or premiums. Special editions, including
personalized covers, excerpts of existing books, and corporate
imprints, can be created in large quantities for special needs.

For more information in the USA write to Special
Markets/Premium Sales, 1745 Broadway, MD 6–2, New York,
NY 10019, or e-mail specialmarkets@randomhouse.com.

In the United Kingdom contact Kuperard publishers at the
address at the top of this page.

Cover image: Edinburgh Castle. © *Louise McGilviray / Fotolia.com*
Images on the following pages reproduced under Creative Commons License
Attribution 2.0, 2.5, and 3.0: 13 © Morgens Engelund; 21 © Kjetil Bjørnsrud;
46 © Chabacano; 50 © Scottish Government; 76 © David Ball;
78 (bottom) © David Monniaux; 94 © Stuart Caie; 95 © Dave Wheeler;
98 © Jeremy Keith; 100, 106, and 133 © Dave Souza; 102 © Edinburgh Blog;
112 © Nicor; 113 © Elitre; 118 © James F. Perry; 121 © John R. from Scotland;
127 © Steve from Washington, DC, USA; 131 (top) © Sue Jackson, (bottom)
© Nicolas17; 141 © Jamesfcarter; 142 © Vidario;144 © StaraBlazkova;
and 147 © Paddy Patterson from Glasgow

About the Author

JOHN H. SCOTNEY is a writer, college lecturer, and former BBC producer. He was the BBC's head of drama in Northern Ireland and later head of BBC TV's Drama Script Unit. He has written books and articles about literature and the media, and written and directed numerous programs for the BBC, many on Scottish themes. He is a former chair of the Writers' Guild of Great Britain, deputy chair of the National Poetry Society, and a fellow of the Royal Society of Arts.

John Scotney's second name, Halcrow, is from the Shetland Islands in the far north, from where everyone else in Britain can be seen as a Sassenach, or southerner. His family is involved in many aspects of Scottish life. His son is head chef for Loch Fyne, the famous fish restaurant group; a cousin in Edinburgh led a team revising the city's transportation system; and the wife of another cousin is a member of the body responsible for the upkeep of remote Iona Abbey, the birthplace of Scots Christianity and the burial place of Scotland's ancient kings.

**The Culture Smart! series is continuing to expand.
For further information and latest titles visit
www.culturesmartguides.com**

The publishers would like to thank **CultureSmart!**Consulting for its help in researching and developing the concept for this series.

CultureSmart!Consulting creates tailor-made seminars and consultancy programs to meet a wide range of corporate, public-sector, and individual needs. Whether delivering courses on multicultural team building in the USA, preparing Chinese engineers for a posting in Europe, training call-center staff in India, or raising the awareness of police forces to the needs of diverse ethnic communities, it provides essential, practical, and powerful skills worldwide to an increasingly international workforce.

For details, visit www.culturesmartconsulting.com

CultureSmart!Consulting and **CultureSmart!** guides have both contributed to and featured regularly in the weekly travel program "Fast Track" on BBC World TV.

contents

contents

contents

Map of Scotland

introduction

The Highlands on a crisp, bright day: the blue deepwater loch, glens, castles, great stags tossing their antlers, heather-clad moors, snow-clad mountains, kilt-clad pipers, eagles high above. For the romantically inclined, such a vision of Scotland may be enough—but anyone doing business in Scotland or really trying to understand the country soon becomes aware that the true heartland is the central Lowlands. Here the vast majority live, here the people of Scotland have built the cities, the universities, and the factories, here they have fought most of their battles, crowned kings, written poetry, music, novels, tracts, and theses, and made scientific and technological breakthroughs.

Though this book says quite a lot about the Highlands, since they are important to the Scots' self-image, it concentrates more on these latter aspects of Scottish life. For it is not so much about the scenery as about the people: it looks at who the Scots really are, how they see life and live it, and how they conduct business.

The cartoon Scotsman is a whisky-swigging, highland-flinging, kilted clansman, so tightfisted he has a padlock on his sporran. And the womenfolk? They stay at home in the croft, salting the porridge and raising the *bairns*, obeying their menfolk, endlessly weaving cloth in the same changeless clan tartan, a monotony only relieved by gutting the fish when the catch is in. Absurd, of course—but there are other stereotypes too, more credible, and often accepted. The Lowlanders: honest, thrifty, hardworking, decent people, careful with money; perhaps a little stiff, strict even; grave citizens with the puritan values of Presbyterianism. Glaswegians: wild men, hard-drinking and drunken, cursing and gambling, spendthrift, mad, violent—a tartan army spreading mayhem. The Highlander: the craggy, bearded sage in shaggy tweeds, slow and clear of speech, wise in the ways of the tides and rivers, the birds and the fish, and the difficult bunker at the eleventh hole.

If there is a grain of truth in these figures, they are two-dimensional and far from typical. Modern Scotland is home to technicians and technocrats, writers, hoteliers, wind farmers, musicians, bold soldiers, overbold investment bankers, the oil and gas industry, skilled doctors, artists, inventors and learned professors, and women everywhere in every sort of job: in 2008 more than half of the jobs in Scotland were held by women.

This book will show you how the geography of the country, including the Highlands and remote islands, has shaped the Scottish people. It explains why their history is important to them, and gives an insight into their values and attitudes, their home life, their business practices, their faults and virtues, their world view and beliefs. It offers practical advice on what to expect and how to behave in different circumstances, and how, perhaps, to gain their acceptance as a friend and colleague.

Key Facts

Official Name	Scotland	Part of the United Kingdom of Great Britain and Northern Ireland
Capital City	Edinburgh (pop. 448,500)	
Main Cities	Glasgow (pop. 575,000), Aberdeen (pop. 202,000), Dundee (pop. 145,000), Inverness (pop. 137,000), Stirling (pop. 86,212)	
Area	31,510 sq. miles (78,772 sq. km) in area, including 609 sq. miles (1,577 sq. km) of freshwater lochs; 275 miles (440 km) from north to south, and varying in breadth between 24 (41 km) and 154 miles (248 km)	
Climate	Temperate. The mean air temp. is 2°F (1.25°C) below that of England, while av. rainfall is 15 in. higher in any year.	There is no month in which av. temps. in Scotland fall below the freezing point.
Currency	Pound sterling. All Scottish banks have the right to print their own notes.	Three do so: Bank of Scotland, Royal Bank of Scotland, and Clydesdale Bank.
Population	5.1 million	
Ethnic Mix	88% of Scotland's population are Scottish-born and 98% are white.	Indians, Bangladeshis, and Pakistanis total 50,000; Chinese 1,600; and other groups are insignificant.
Language	English, with many dialect words, spoken by all Scots	Additionally, Gaelic is spoken by 60,000 people.

Religion	Scotland is traditionally a Christian nation; 65% at the 2001 census.	The national Church is Presbyterian; 2,146,251 at the 2001 census. Roman Catholics, 803,732; other Christians, 344,562. Approx. 40,000 Muslims
Government	Government is in four tiers: the Scottish Parliament in Edinburgh, responsible for most aspects of Scottish life; the National Parliament in Westminster, responsible for defense, foreign affairs, and taxation; and the European Parliament in Brussels with certain powers vested in the European Union. A secretary of state for Scotland based in London is part of the British cabinet. There are 32 directly elected local authorities that receive much of their funding from the Scottish Executive.	
Media	Several satellite and cable channels. Two BBC TV channels with programs of Scottish interest and a commercial station (STV)	Digital Gaelic station. As well as UK-wide radio channels there are BBC Radio Scotland and BBC Gaelic radio services and local indep. radio stations.
Press	Scotland has over 80 newspapers serving local communities and three major national papers, together with Scottish editions of several of the main UK newspapers.	
Electricity	240 volts, 50 Hz	Flat three-pronged plugs used
Video/TV	PAL system	
Telephone	Country code 44	
Internet Domain	.uk	
Time Zone	GMT	+ 1 hr. in summer

chapter one

LAND & PEOPLE

Scotland is a constituent part of the United Kingdom that four hundred or so years ago was an independent nation, and that might become one again. It has its own legal system and Church, and its own parliament with substantial powers of self-government.

GEOGRAPHY

Scotland is nearly two-thirds the size of England but its population of some 5.1 million is a tenth of England's, and of those, 2.5 million are crammed into the industrial southwest. A geological fracture, the Highland Boundary Fault, separates two markedly different landscapes. To the north, bisected by the Great Glen with its string of deep lochs (lakes), are the Highlands, an area of breathtaking views and hard, ancient rock whose heather-covered moorland and stern mountains stretch eastward toward Aberdeen and southward along Loch Lomond to the Clyde.

In the far north and west are 750 wind- and rain-swept islands, 130 of them inhabited, with a beauty and appeal of their own. Southeast of the Fault are softer sedimentary rocks creating rounded hills and fertile farmlands. The Lowlands of mid-Scotland are the site of the former coal and iron industry, and run diagonally across the country. They take in Edinburgh, Glasgow, and the Clyde industrial belt, and extend northward almost to Aberdeen.

Heading south again brings rich agricultural land and, beyond that, bleak hills and infertile moorland. This is the bloodstained border country, with its cruel fortresses and ruined abbeys. The Highlands cover half of Scotland and have half a million inhabitants. The central Lowlands and the Borders are home to the other 4.5 million Scots.

CLIMATE

Nowhere in Scotland is far from the sea, and this influences both people and climate. The North Atlantic is famously unpredictable, and it produces equally unpredictable weather that can change in a matter of moments. The climate is also surprisingly temperate, however, thanks to a strong ocean current carrying the warm waters of the Gulf

Stream northward. The mountains can be cold and the wind bitter, while the relatively high latitude of northern Scotland makes for long winter nights counterbalanced by long summer days. Scotland is wetter than England, with three quarters of an inch (0.2 mm) or more of rain falling 250 days a year. The Western Highlands are the wettest, their annual rainfall being 180 inches (4,570 mm). In winter rain turns to snow and the central Highlands have 36 to 105 days of snow a year; the mild west coast, on the other hand, has at most a few days and sometimes none at all. Scotland is a land of contrasts, and nowhere more so than in its weather and its people.

Inshriach Nursery near Aviemore in the Cairngorms specializes in Alpine flowers; at the Logan Botanic Gardens on Mull, subtropical plants thrive.

WHO ARE THE SCOTS?
Five peoples formed the nation that came together as Scotland: Picts, Gaels, Britons, Angles, and Norsemen. Each spoke a different language, though the language of the Angles would come to dominate the midlands and south, and Gaelic the north and west. Even today about 1 percent of Scots are Gaelic speakers, and there are television and radio stations that broadcast in this language.

Neighbors too, on all sides, played their part in shaping Scotland and the Scots. England—rich, powerful, and greedy—to the south; France and the Netherlands to the east; Scandinavia northward, across icy, treacherous seas; Celtic

Ireland a handful of miles to the west; then west again, way beyond but beckoning, Nova Scotia, Canada, and the USA; and farther still, the wide world. Each helped mold this hardy, practical, people, who are also romantic, loyal, hardheaded, softhearted, God-fearing, and sometimes foolhardy, but always "their own man."

A BRIEF HISTORY
Prehistory
Eight thousand years ago, Scotland's minute population scraped a living as hunter-gatherers. Three thousand years later, Skara Brae on Orkney had sophisticated stone houses with stone cupboards, stone seats, stone beds, hearths, tables, and drains, matched on the mainland by chambered tombs reminiscent of Mycenaean Greece. Another three thousand years later the Romans came and saw but did not conquer, instead building Hadrian's Wall and withdrawing behind it.

Picts and Scots

Archaeological evidence reveals that the Picts
were in Scotland when the Romans came. First
mentioned by the name "Picts" in a Latin text of
297 CE, they were skilled in metalwork and stone
carving, but no one knows what language they
spoke. Then there are the Scots. To confuse
matters, the "Scots" are Irish in culture and
language: "Scoti" is their Latin name, but they
called themselves "Gaels." Artistically gifted
craftsmen, this Celtic people established a
kingdom in the west: Dál Riata. For centuries they
fought the Picts north and east of them, the
Vikings, each other, and their Irish cousins.

The Coming of Christianity

Many Scottish people have strong religious
convictions, and the Gaels' great gift to Scotland is

Christianity. After the fall of the
Roman Empire in the West, Ireland
was a haven of what was left of
Western civilization and Christianity:
a land of "saints and scholars." One
of these Irish saints, Saint Columba,
landed in the Western Isles in 563 CE,
founding a monastery on Iona. From
the Gaelic west this Irish form of
Christianity spread across Scotland;
in due course Glasgow gained its first
bishop, Saint Mungo, and by the late
seventh century the whole country
was Christian.

Celtic Christianity differs from Roman
Catholicism. It is said that the Roman Church

reverenced the authoritative Saint Peter and the
Celtic Church the sensitive Saint John, and that
"the Celtic Church gave love while the Roman
Church gave law." Be that as it may, the Celts at
least theoretically submitted to papal authority
at the Synod of Whitby in 663 CE, though Celtic
religious practices continued until the eleventh
century, when Queen Margaret finally established
the victory of Roman Catholicism over the old
Celtic Church. Even today in the Scottish attitude
to religion there remains something of this
ancient faith, which put the individual conscience
before the bishop's ordinance.

Britons and Angles
The fertile southern Lowlands were home to
another group of Celts. The Britons lived in hill
towns, one of them ruled by Coel Hen—Old King
Cole himself. They spoke a different language,
Brythonic, akin to Welsh, and had strong links
with Roman Britain. Their kingdom of
Strathclyde in the southwest would survive until
the eleventh century, and the people of the region
still boast a distinct identity. Meanwhile, a
Germanic tribe, the Angles, came from across the
sea, occupied northeast England and created the
kingdom of Northumbria. In the seventh century
the Northumbrians seized southeast Scotland,
including the town to which they gave the name
"Edinburgh," after their king, Edwin. The Gaels
called these newcomers "Sassenachs" (Saxons),
and they spoke a form of what would become
English, though one that would always differ
from the English of southern England.

Norsemen

In the ninth and tenth centuries, King Robert
MacAlpin and his grandson Constantine united the
Picts and Scots. On a hill at Scone near Perth they
were enthroned rather than crowned, being seated
on a sandstone block called the Stone of Destiny, as
would become the normal practice for Scottish kings.
The joint kingdom was named "Alba" in Gaelic.

The two peoples had come together to confront
the savage Norsemen: pagan Scandinavian
sea-rovers who sailed their long ships
as far and wide as America, the
Mediterranean, and deep into
Russia. In England they rebuilt
York, in Ireland they founded
Dublin, and in France they seized the whole
peninsula still named after them: Normandy.

From 750 CE onward these "Vikings" raided and
then colonized Shetland, Orkney, and Caithness.
Orkney and Shetland would not become part of
Scotland until 1468, and even in the twenty-first
century they have a noticeable affinity to Norway in
their music and folklore. There are still Orcadians
and Shetlanders who regard Scotland as a foreign
country. Other Norsemen slaughtered the monks of
Iona and seized the Western Isles, holding them until
the thirteenth century.

At last the Viking threat, which had seemed about
to overwhelm Scotland, was contained, and in 1016
King Malcolm II defeated the Angles at the battle of
Carham, carrying his border south to the River
Tweed. Some time later, Strathclyde was absorbed.
So, in the eleventh century mainland Scotland
became united for the first time, though the Western

Isles, Orkney, and Shetland still owed allegiance to Norway, and English kings from Canute to Edward I would assert suzerainty over their Scots neighbors.

Heroes and Villains

In the words of Robert Louis Stevenson, "The mark of a Scot is that he remembers and cherishes the memory of his forebears, good or bad; and there burns alive in him a sense of identity with the dead even to the twentieth generation."

A parade of larger-than-life characters struggling with England, innovating, winning and losing, building and tearing down, make up Scotland's vision of its past, and Scotland's heroes and villains are central to the Scottish sense of nationhood.

Unbeaten on the Bus

A tale is told of a Scottish bus driver taking a group of Americans on a tour. Every now and again he would point out the scene of a notable English defeat. "And there you see Bannockburn, where a wee Scots army destroyed an English army many times its size," he would say, and further on he would describe how General Cope was crushed at Prestonpans, or Killikrankie, where the Marquis of Dundee… and so on. The bus stopped for a break and everyone got out. One of the Americans came up to the driver. "Excuse me for asking," he said, "but didn't the English ever beat the Scots?" The driver took a long drag of his cigarette, thought for a moment, and then replied: "Never on my bus, pal."

Duncan and Macbeth

Duncan, the second king of all Scotland, was not the kindly old fellow of Shakespeare's play, but young, headstrong, brutal—he killed his own grandfather—and incompetent. Macbeth killed Duncan in battle and turned out to be rather a good king who reigned for seventeen years, far longer than Shakespeare's account suggests. According to Shakespeare, Macbeth was defeated by Malcolm Canmore (Bighead) at Dunsinane in 1054; what is less well-known is that he survived for another three years until finally killed near Aberdeen by Malcolm and his English allies. Shakespeare lived in the reign of James I of England, who traced his ancestry back to Duncan—which could explain the playwright's jaundiced view of Macbeth and his wife. Her name, incidentally, was Gruoch, though curiously Shakespeare never mentions this.

The House of Canmore

Malcolm founded a dynasty lasting two centuries. The House of Canmore was bound to England by ties of marriage, often relied on support from the new Norman rulers of England, and equally often fought them. Norman lords and gentry were invited to settle, and today's great Scottish landowners are predominantly of Norman-English origin. Under the Canmores, trade flourished, trading towns called *burghs* were founded, and the first Scottish coins were issued. "Scotia" became the standard term for Scotland. Alexander III fought off a Norwegian invasion in 1263, and Scotland regained the Western Isles from Norway.

Alexander's daughter married the Norwegian king's grandson, and in due course, in 1286, their infant daughter became Queen of Scotland.

The Wars of Liberation: Wallace and Bruce
Unfortunately, Margaret, the "Maid of Norway," was only three. In 1290 she sailed to her new realm but died on the voyage. King Edward I of England had guaranteed the survival of Scotland as an independent country, and was asked to arbitrate between the various contenders for the throne. He chose John Balliol, who was set upon the stone in 1292, but immediately the English king started treating Balliol as his puppet. The Scots rebelled and were defeated, and Balliol was made to surrender the throne—quite literally, for Edward took the Stone of Scone south to Westminster Abbey. For ten years England ruled Scotland, until a mere commoner, William Wallace, rose in arms and beat the

English at the Battle of Stirling Bridge. Wallace was knighted and governed Scotland briefly; then, risking battle when he should not have done, he was defeated. Two years later Wallace was captured, taken to London, and cruelly executed.

Six months later still, Robert the Bruce, having initially submitted to Edward I, declared himself King and was crowned at Scone in 1306. At first he too was beaten, at the Battle of Methven, and fled for his life. Legend has it that, hiding in a cave, he watched a spider fail to build its web many times until finally it succeeded. Bruce too persevered. In 1307 Edward I, the "Hammer of the Scots," died, to be succeeded by the weaker Edward II. Bruce ruthlessly suppressed all opposition and united Scotland behind himself. In 1314, by choosing his ground well and skillfully deploying his small force of spearmen, he routed Edward's much larger army at the Battle of Bannockburn, and Scotland was free—though it would be fourteen years before the English conceded Scots independence.

Wallace the bold patriot, the "man of the people" who lost and was tragically martyred, and the persistent, pragmatic Bruce, who was cannily victorious, are iconic Scottish heroes, each reflecting something in the Scots character. Both were of Norman/Scottish stock—a formidable mix!

The Declaration of Arbroath
In 1320 King Robert wrote a letter to the Pope, sealed by all the leading Scottish lords, proclaiming the new independence. It is known as the Declaration of Arbroath, and it states: "as long as but a hundred of us remain alive, never will we on any conditions be brought under English rule. It is in truth not for glory, nor riches, nor honours that we fight, but for freedom—for that alone, which no honest man gives up but with life itself."

Certain Inalienable Rights ...
Some Americans see the Declaration of Arbroath
as the forerunner of the Declaration of
Independence. The USA now celebrates "Tartan
Day" on the anniversary of the Declaration of
Arbroath being written: April 6.

The Fourteenth Century

The fighting continued. In 1346 Bruce's son
David invaded England, nearly losing everything
his father had won by his defeat and capture at
Neville's Cross. The Black Death came, halving
Europe's population, but the warfare went on.
At the "Burnt Candlemass" of 1356, English
troops ravaged Edinburgh. Nevertheless, by the
time David died, all Europe acknowledged him
as Scotland's King. Because he was childless the
succession passed to the descendants of his elder
sister, Marjorie, wife to Scotland's hereditary
steward. Their son became Robert II in 1371.
And so begins the house of "Steward," whose
links with Scotland were to last until Bonnie
Prince Charlie's fateful campaign of 1745.

The Early Stuarts

The late medieval period saw England tied up in
war with France until the English nobles started
slaughtering each other in the Wars of the Roses.
In Scotland the Lord of the Isles, successor to the
Norse rulers, was virtually independent, as were
the Black Douglases in the south. James I spent
eighteen years in English captivity, but on his
return he and his successors gradually brought

these overmighty subjects to heel, though both James and his grandson James III were to die at the hands of their own nobles. Parliament was developed as a counterpoise to the great nobles, and the marriage of James III to Margaret of Denmark in 1468 finally brought the Orkneys and Shetlands into the kingdom. Scotland's first university, Saint Andrews, was founded in 1413, to be followed by the University of Glasgow in 1451.

Curiosity Killed the King

In 1460, James II was an early victim of the Scottish spirit of inquiry—he was investigating how his new cannon worked when it blew up and killed him.

Flodden

James IV (1488–1513) did much to subdue the nobles: the Lord of the Isles had finally fallen, and James took the title to himself. Their fall meant the Gaels of the Highlands and Islands began to be seen as second-class citizens.

James's reign was a time of learning and literacy: Aberdeen University dates from 1495, the Edinburgh College of Surgeons from 1506, and the first printing press in Edinburgh from 1507; in 1496 a groundbreaking law required all prosperous landowners to send their eldest sons to school. From this foundation the Scots would later become the most literate people in northern Europe, and the Scottish respect and zeal for education endures to this day.

In England, the bellicose young Henry VIII was eager for war with France. James IV tried to maintain the peace but failed, and Scotland's "Auld Alliance" with the French drew him into invading England.

While Henry VIII was fighting his futile war in France, it fell to his wife, Catherine of Aragon, whom he had made Regent, to oppose the Scottish threat. The campaign she launched proved considerably more successful than her husband's. In 1513 the Duke of Surrey decisively beat the Scots, killing James himself and the flower of his chivalry at the Battle of Flodden Field. In the moving lament "The Flowers of the Forest," Scottish pipers still bewail the death of their hero king. Queen Catherine sent James's bloodstained coat to Henry in France.

Death Chant

There is a superstition in Scotland that the piper should only play "The Flowers of the Forest" at funerals. To do otherwise is to court his own death or that of his patron.

When the new king of Scotland, James V, grew up he, too, invaded England and he, too, was defeated—at Solway Moss in 1542. He died in the same year, passing his crown to his week-old daughter, Mary, named after her French mother, Mary of Guise. Mary of Guise became the effective ruler of Scotland in her daughter's name and was officially named Regent in 1554.

Mary, Queen of Scots' Childhood

Henry VIII, now near death, wanted his heir, Edward, to marry Mary. A series of English invasions, known as the "Rough Wooing," resulted in Mary, aged five, being sent to safety in France, where her Guise uncles brought her up as a Frenchwoman. The French could not pronounce "Steward," so she became Mary Stuart, and in 1558, at the age of fifteen, she made a great marriage with the Dauphin Francis, the heir to the French throne.

"The Monstrous Regiment of Women"

In 1559, King Henry II of France died of injuries sustained while jousting with the captain of his

Scots Guard. Suddenly the world was at the feet of a pretty, willful sixteen-year-old who had spent her life pampered in the French court and now found herself Queen of both France and Scotland. In England that same year, Mary's cousin Elizabeth was crowned Queen, and Scotland saw the return from exile of a middle-aged clergyman with a long beard who strongly disapproved of women holding any power: John Knox. In 1558 he wrote a book on the subject entitled *The First Blast of the Trumpet Against the Monstrous Regiment of Women*.

The Scottish Reformation

Forty-one years earlier, Luther had published his *Ninety-Five Theses*, protesting against papal abuses. Thanks to the new printing presses his ideas had spread rapidly, and Protestant and Catholic armies had crisscrossed Europe killing and pillaging in the name of the Risen Christ, while Henry VIII had replaced the Pope with himself as head of the English Church. Protestant ideas reached Scotland quite early and gradually gained ground. A Protestant uprising against the Regency in 1546 led by Knox was suppressed and the rebels were chained to oars in French galleys. After the galleys Knox went to England and Geneva, home of the strictest form of Protestantism, Calvinism. He would become the hero of the Scottish Reformation and the epitome of the stern Calvinist man of God still encountered in Scotland.

In 1557 a group of nobles calling themselves the "Lords of Congregation" and comprising the Earls of Argyll, Glencairn, and Morton, Lord Lorne, and Erskine of Dun, met and signed "the Covenant," a document upholding the Protestant cause. Knox's preaching now won many more converts. In 1559 Mary of Guise was deposed as Regent; she died in 1560. That same year, the Scottish parliament severed all links with Rome and banned the Catholic Mass.

In 1561, the Reformation carried the pioneering work of James IV yet further. Knox's new Protestant Church of Scotland embarked on a program of education, establishing a school in every parish, a remarkable initiative whose benefits are still felt four hundred and fifty years later.

Witch Hunts

While condemning Catholic "superstition,"
Scottish Protestants were themselves
superstitiously obsessed with rooting out witches.
To Scotland's discredit, over four thousand alleged
witches were burnt or hanged between the mid-
fifteenth and mid-eighteenth centuries. Rowan
trees, believed to be a protection against witches,
can still be seen outside older cottages.

Mary as Queen of Scots

Things now started to go badly wrong for the
young Queen of Scots. Francis II died after a brief
reign, to be succeeded as King of France by his
ten-year-old brother Charles IX. The supporters
of the new French king had no time for Mary or
her Guise relations, so in 1561 Mary returned, in
all but birth a French aristocrat, to her newly

Protestant realm and her
chilly palace of Holyrood.
Knox did all he could to
show her the error of her
Catholic faith, but could
not move her. Mary,
though, had to accept the
reality of the Scottish
Reformation while
remaining herself a
Catholic. In 1565 she
married Lord Darnley, and
they had a son called
James, but Darnley was jealous of Mary's Italian
secretary Riccio, and murdered him. Unable to

forgive Darnley, Mary came under the spell of the handsome Earl of Bothwell. In 1567 the house where Darnley was staying was blown up. Darnley was found to have been strangled beforehand, however, probably by Bothwell. When, shortly afterward, Mary tactlessly married Bothwell, the Protestant nobles were furious and forced her to abdicate in favor of her baby son, who became James VI.

Mary raised a force but, defeated, fled to her cousin Elizabeth in England. Elizabeth refused to meet her, imprisoned her in Fotheringay Castle, and eventually in 1587 had her beheaded. In death, Mary, Queen of Scots is the great Scots tragic heroine, cruelly betrayed by her English cousin. This is not a wholly fair judgment: it was the Scots who threw her out, the Spanish Armada was virtually on the horizon, and Mary was certainly plotting against Elizabeth. James, now ruling Scotland in his own right, did little to help his mother—Elizabeth was unlikely to have children, and he was the heir apparent to the English throne. The Armada came and went, and in 1589 James married Anne of Denmark, bravely sailing over the North Sea to collect her. He was an able King of Scotland but was arguably less successful in his next role.

"The Wisest Fool in Christendom"
In 1603 Elizabeth died and James VI of Scotland was crowned James I of England, sitting on a throne that contained the Stone of Scone. After the penny-pinching poverty of his Scottish court he felt he had arrived in a land of milk and

honey. James was an intelligent man who wrote an impassioned attack on smoking four hundred years ahead of its time, but he has had a bad press: the French ambassador called him "the

wisest fool in Christendom," and Sir Walter Scott later ridiculed him in *The Fortunes of Nigel*. James was clumsy, pompous, and undignified, but he genuinely loved the arts. Shakespeare, John Donne, Francis Bacon, and Ben Jonson all flourished under his patronage, and he was personally responsible for commissioning the magnificent Authorized Version of the Bible.

Despite its absentee king, Scotland prospered, not least because James finally put down the Border Reivers: families of brutal outlaws, Scots and English alike, holed up in grim towers in "the debatable lands," living by cattle rustling and "blackmail" ("mail" meant "rent," so blackmail was "black rent," or protection money). While Protestants and Catholics tore each other apart in Europe, James—who once remarked, "I could never allow it in my conscience that the blood of any man should be spilt for diversity of religion"—gave his two kingdoms nearly twenty-five years of almost total peace.

Remember, Remember, the Fifth of November
James was tolerant toward Catholics, but less so
after November 5, 1605, when Guy Fawkes and his
fellow Catholic conspirators tried to blow him up,
together with both Houses of Parliament. James's
ire was understandable, since his father, Lord
Darnley, had himself been the victim of another
"gunpowder plot." Throughout Britain the fifth of
November is known as "Guy Fawkes Night," when
fireworks are set off and Fawkes himself is burned
in effigy on a bonfire.

The "Bishops' Wars"

Though Scotland and England were now united
under a single ruler, hostilities involving the two
countries would continue for many more years.
Charles I, short, shy, and arrogant, became King
in 1625. He tended to forget he was King of
Scotland, until in 1637 the issue of religion
divided the two peoples. Charles had tried to
impose the English liturgy and Anglican-style
bishops on the Calvinist Church of Scotland, but
when the Liturgy was read in Edinburgh there was
a riot. An old woman called Jenny Geddes is said
to have thrown the stool she was sitting on at the
Dean, shouting: "Out thou false thief! Dost thou
say the Mass at my lug [ear]?"

Over three days in February 1638, Scottish
Presbyterian notables signed the National
Covenant promising to uphold "true religion."
They then expelled the Scottish bishops. Charles
recalled the English Parliament for the first time
in eleven years in an attempt to raise troops to

force the Scots to submit.
Meanwhile, the Scots
recruited an army, so
that when Charles
failed to persuade
the English
Parliament to give
him any money, he
had to make peace.

Charles did
manage to raise an
army of sorts in 1640,
but unhappily for him,

Scottish gentlemen had for years supplemented
their meager incomes by service as soldiers in the
highly trained Protestant forces that had been
fighting all over Europe. Several of them, notably
Lord Leven and Sir David Leslie, served as senior
officers. The Scots professionals swept aside the
King's forces at the Battle of Newburn and
occupied Newcastle and Durham almost
unopposed.

The Civil Wars
The First Civil War, 1642–46
In England, relations between Charles and
Parliament were becoming ever more hostile.
In 1642 Parliament tried to gain control of the
nation's armed forces; the King raised his
standard in Nottingham and declared war. Many
on the Parliamentary side were good Protestants,
and in 1643 they persuaded the Scots to invade
by apparently promising to make England
Presbyterian—and by offering them money.

In 1644 the Scots, under their veteran General Lord Leven, participated in the battle of Marston Moor, which lost the King the north of England and in effect lost him the war. For the remainder of the war northern England would be held for Parliament by a Scottish garrison under Sir David Leslie.

Montrose

In September 1644 one of the great Scots romantic heroes appeared, but too late. The Marquis of Montrose, handsome poet and daring leader, "raised the Highlands for the King," though in truth at first his "Highlanders" were largely Irish MacDonalds—which was as well, because the Highlanders themselves tended to pack up and go home after a battle, win or lose. Within a single year Montrose won a series of seemingly impossible victories against the Earl of Argyll, whose forces, made up of Covenanters and his own Clan Campbell, greatly outnumbered the 2,000 or so Scottish Royalists. Scotland was at Montrose's feet.

In England, however, the war was lost. King Charles was actually making his way north to join Montrose when he learned that Sir David Leslie, having withdrawn his experienced Scottish troops from northern England, had quashed the Marquis's ramshackle little Royalist army at Philiphaugh. This Scottish Civil War had not been chivalrous: Montrose's men had brutally sacked Perth and in retaliation, despite Leslie's protests, the beaten clansmen, along with their wives and children, were butchered by Argyll's men.

Montrose escaped, but in 1646 Charles surrendered to the Scots regiments at Newark, who sold him to the English Parliament in return for arrears of pay.

The Second and Third Civil Wars

In a remarkable turnabout, less than two years later, when more fighting broke out in the so-called Second Civil War, a Scots army appeared in England to fight on behalf of Charles. Oliver Cromwell, in his first independent command, caught up with it at Preston and demolished it. Then, in 1649, the English Parliament beheaded Charles, who died with dignity and courage. The Scots were none too pleased about the English executing a Scottish king without asking them first, so when the dead King's son appeared in Scotland, they crowned him Charles II.

Argyll officiated at the coronation, for the Scots had always seen themselves as fighting against the King's evil English ministers rather than against the King himself.

Young Charles II accepted the Covenant, and the Scots were taken in by his protestations. Montrose arrived to join him but unfortunately attacked his old enemies the Covenanters, who were now the new King's friends. He was executed by Argyll, who still hated his old enemy.

Cromwell defeated Leslie at Dunbar, after which, against Leslie's advice, a last Scots army invaded England and was crushed by Cromwell at Worcester. Young Charles went on the run and escaped to France.

The Usurpation and the Restoration
During the ten years known as "the
Commonwealth" in England or "the Usurpation"
in Scotland, things went rather well for that
defeated country: "true religion" thrived and
prosperity returned under Cromwell's governor,
General Monck. Argyll returned to his old
allegiance, submitted to General Monck in 1652,
and helped put down a minor Royalist uprising in
1653. In truth only the Scots' pride was hurt, but
pride means a lot to the Scots.

Then, in 1660, a year after Cromwell's death,
Monck marched south, chewing tobacco and
giving no one any idea what his plans were.
Thanks to Monck, by the end of 1660 Scotland,
like England, had its King again: a charming,
witty, wholly unreliable man who seemed to have
no recollection of ever having signed any
Covenant. Charles II never visited Scotland again,
though he did have Argyll executed for treason.

The Glorious Revolution
Charles II died in 1685. His brother was now King
James VII of Scotland and James II of England.
James was a Roman Catholic and when his ally,
Louis XIV, launched a campaign of savage
persecution against the French Protestants, or
"Huguenots," many fled to Scotland and England.
Could the same happen in Scotland?

James had a daughter, Mary, married to the
Dutch ruler William, Prince of Orange, a staunch
Calvinist and Louis's sworn enemy. In 1688 the
English magnates invited William and Mary to
take over the throne—without consulting the

Scots, of course. James fled. After the so-called "Glorious Revolution," William and Mary became joint rulers and the Scottish Parliament restored Presbyterianism. But William put the Netherlands' interests first. The Scots were now playing second fiddle to the English, who were in turn playing second fiddle to the Dutch. Not all Scots welcomed this situation, and the Highlanders rose under Viscount Dundee. They won a heroic victory at Killiecrankie in 1689, largely because the Scots/English Redcoats facing them couldn't get their new bayonets fixed before they were hacked to pieces by the Highland broadswords. Dundee was killed, though, and as Montrose had found, the Highlanders, regardless of having won, melted away.

Glencoe

One of these disappearing Highlanders was Alasdair MacIain MacDonald of Glencoe, an old rogue with a dreadful reputation as bandit. On his way home from Killiecrankie he raided Campbell territory and burned Achallader Castle. A pardon was offered to all clan chiefs who took the oath of loyalty to King William by the last day of 1691, but old Alasdair was five days late. The King himself decided to make an example of the MacDonalds of Glencoe by billeting government troops—in fact a regiment of the "British" army raised from Clan Campbell—in their cottages. The MacDonalds treated them hospitably, but after ten days the soldiers received written orders to kill every MacDonald under seventy—over three hundred people. In fact thirty-eight people, including Alasdair and his wife, were murdered in their beds, though others died of cold after fleeing into the mountains. The Glencoe Massacre of February 13, 1692, burns in Scotland's memory to this day. To Highlanders, the soldiers' abuse of the MacDonalds' hospitality was at least as grave a crime as the murders themselves.

The Act of Union

King William realized that James, now exiled in France, might return to Scotland to reclaim his throne, and to prevent this he urged a formal union of England and Scotland. After William died, his successor, Queen Anne, also promoted the union. Plenty of canny Scots entrepreneurs were in favor: England was rich, especially now that a Scot, William Patterson, had founded the Bank of England; Scotland was poor, especially since many Scottish merchants had lost their fortunes on a disastrous colonial venture called the Darien Scheme devised by that same William Patterson. A treaty was drawn up: the two nations would combine their flags and share a parliament, but Scotland would keep its own Church and its own legal system. The Scots Parliament accepted the Treaty of Union and voted itself into oblivion for two hundred and ninety years, and the United

Kingdom was born on May 1, 1707. However, partly because they felt railroaded into it, the Act of Union was unpopular with many patriotic Scots.

The Jacobites

When James died in 1701 his son James Francis Edward took up the Stuart cause. In Latin James is "Jacobus," and his followers were known as the Jacobites, while he himself became known as the "Old Pretender."

Mountains and Molehills

King William died from injuries sustained when his horse stumbled over a molehill, and for many years Scottish Jacobites would raise their glasses to "the little gentleman in black velvet."

Queen Anne died without an heir in 1714, to be succeeded by her cousin, George, the Elector of Hanover—a Protestant German prince who spoke no English. In 1715 the Earl of Mar denounced the Act of Union and proclaimed the reign of King James VIII. Highlanders flocked to join him and they soon captured Perth, but towns south of the River Tay stayed loyal to the Union.

The Battle of Sheriffmuir was indecisive, and government reinforcements flooded in. James Edward landed at Peterhead to find his forces retreating in the face of superior odds. In February 1716 he proved himself his father's son by leaving them in the lurch. The Highlanders drifted away as usual, and George I remained monarch of the United Kingdom.

Bonnie Prince Charlie

Thirty years later, in August 1745, James's son, an Italian-born, half-Polish Catholic whose full name was Charles Edward Louis John Casimir Sylvester Severino Maria Stuart, decided to make another

attempt at a Stuart restoration on behalf of his father. The "Young Pretender" was a bolder and more charismatic figure than his father, and when he landed on the little island of Eriskay he became another Scottish hero as "Bonnie Prince Charlie."

The Highlanders didn't exactly rush to join him, but enough arrived eventually and Edinburgh fell to them.

The Jacobites routed General Cope's Redcoats at Prestopans and once again a Scottish army invaded England. It got as far south as Derby. King George II panicked and seriously thought about going home to Hanover. However, the clansmen, too, wanted to go home, and many of them actually did leave. Presented with a choice, very few of the English showed any desire to throw in their lot with this foreign prince and his ever-declining band of ragged Highlanders. The remaining Jacobites plodded back to Inverness without a battle.

In Scotland, after a minor success at Falkirk, Prince Charlie's 5,000 ill-equipped clansmen had to face a force of 9,000 regulars commanded by one of the royal princes: William, Duke of Cumberland. The Jacobites were crushed at the Battle of Culloden by Cumberland's drilled and disciplined Redcoats, many of them Campbells or Lowland Scots—contrary to myth, more Scots fought against Bonnie Prince Charlie than for him. Charlie himself, aided by one Flora MacDonald and disguised as her Irish maid, got clean away and ended up back in Rome.

After the battle, "Butcher Cumberland" behaved abominably, killing all the Jacobite wounded and prisoners of war. Laws were passed to destroy the Highland way of life: tartans, plaids, and bagpipes were forbidden, except to those— and there were many—willing to serve the King in his new Highland regiments. For many clansmen had actually followed the Young Pretender not out of patriotism, but on their chieftains' orders.

By Any Other Name...
The English named a flower "Sweet William" after
Cumberland; the Highlanders called that same
flower "Stinking Billy."

The Highland Clearances
The clan chiefs lost legal authority and power of
jurisdiction over their clanspeople, but retained
ownership of their lands. In consequence, in the
notorious Highland Clearances from the 1760s
onward, thousands of clansmen were evicted from
their patches of bare farmland by these same
chieftains or their agents, and replaced by sheep,
which were more profitable. To the landlords the
Clearances were "improvements"; for the brutally
uprooted clansmen they were a tragedy.

The Clearances increased in pace throughout
the century, and 1792 was to be christened the
"Year of the Sheep" by resentful Highlanders,
some hundreds of whom were put directly onto
emigration ships bound for Canada. Not all the
dispossessed were Highlanders, however; others
came from the Lowlands, where agricultural
reforms were putting pressure on tenant farmers.
Many of those driven out drifted into the alien
world of the rapidly expanding Lowland cities.
During the nineteenth century the Highland
grouse moors became a profitable source of
income and the Clearances continued unabated
until the 1870s, often only achieved with violence.
The picturesque, empty, heather-covered moors so
appealing to visitors have a bitter significance for
the descendants of the dispossessed.

Emigration

Many emigrated to the colonies or the USA, carrying their resentment with them. Flora MacDonald turned up in Carolina where, with the Highland genius for backing the wrong horse, her family fought for King George III against George Washington.

Not all emigrants were laborers; there were craftsmen, farmers, weavers, skilled metalworkers, and even professional men who rose to positions of importance in the lands they settled.

Scots Ancestry

In all, thirty-two presidents of the United States are of Scots ancestry, and many of the premiers of Canada, Australia, and New Zealand were children and grandchildren of Scottish emigrants. Incidentally, George Washington claimed descent from King Malcolm II.

The Eighteenth Century

The period from the end of the second half of the eighteenth century to the end of the nineteenth was a golden age for Scotland: modern methods of farming were introduced, and for the first time the rule of law covered all Scotland. Between 1756 and 1763 the new, kilted Highland regiments played a heroic role in the Seven Years War, which led to a huge extension of the British Empire in Canada, India, West Africa, and the West Indies. At home, fueled by the labor pool of dispossessed Highlanders and by Scottish inventiveness,

Glasgow and Clydeside led the way in the Industrial Revolution, while in Edinburgh James Craig designed a "New Town" so classically elegant that it became known as the "Athens of the North."

Scotland found its national voice in the poetry of Robert Burns, and the education system initiated by James IV bore fruit in Scotland's "Age of Enlightenment," which dazzled the world.

The Nineteenth Century

In the western Lowlands and on Clydeside, cotton, coal mining, iron making, and shipbuilding grew and grew. Irish labor poured in and the area witnessed the most rapid urbanization in Western Europe; Glasgow expanded far too fast, leading to appalling housing conditions, overcrowding, and disease.

Emigration peaked and Scots were found all over America, in Canada, and in the British Empire in numbers far out of proportion to Scotland's population. They were farmers, laborers, and civil and mechanical engineers, including hundreds of ship's engineers; they were missionaries and explorers (like David Livingston, who was both), common soldiers

and generals, industrialists, merchants who dealt in everything from opium to prefabricated tin chapels, rulers and governors, planters, surveyors, doctors, and inventors such as Alexander Graham Bell, father of the telephone. Even when Scotsmen didn't venture abroad themselves, Scottish money did: Scotland pioneered the investment trust and held enormous investments in North and South America.

Working Conditions
The heroes of the manufacturing explosion, the great industrialists, were also the villains. Scotland was one of the most prosperous parts of the British Empire, but Scottish workers remained among the worst paid in Britain because the influx from Ireland and the Highlands meant labor was over-plentiful. The employers paid as little as they liked, cramming their workforce into stinking tenements. As the nineteenth century progressed, working conditions and living standards did get somewhat better, thanks to the workers themselves forming trade unions (labor unions) to improve their own lot. At the same time, almost unnoticed, British industry was losing its preeminence in the face of German and American competition.

The Twentieth Century
The Scottish cities were rich recruiting grounds for the British Army, and the death toll of the First World War hit hard, to be followed by high unemployment throughout the 1920s and 1930s. Traditional industries such as shipbuilding,

mining, iron, and steel were badly affected by competition and by the Depression.

Though Scottish votes contributed to the Conservative Party winning five of the seven elections in the interwar period, some Scots became disillusioned with the Union. The National Party of Scotland was formed in 1928; in 1934 it became the Scottish National Party (SNP). The first SNP Member of Parliament was elected in 1945, by which time the Second World War had brought a return to full employment and a prosperity that lasted through the 1960s.

Scotland since the 1960s

Between 1970 and 1974 the number of coal mines in Scotland fell by a third and steel production by a fifth, while shipbuilding on the Clyde was in serious trouble. When the Conservative government refused to bail out four shipyards in 1971, trade unionists staged a work-in and occupied the yards.

Then, suddenly, the poor relation won the lottery: oil was discovered in the North Sea. It was as though this discovery jerked Scotland out of its old ways and into the future, so that when recession returned in the early 1980s and early 1990s Scotland threw itself into the new high-tech and service industries that came to replace the old manufacturing base.

GOVERNMENT

The Queen is the head of state of the United Kingdom, but her role is purely ceremonial. The real head of the British government is the prime minister, who is the leader of whichever political party wins the most seats in the House of Commons in general elections. The British Parliament at Westminster has 72 elected Scottish members, out of over 600 MPs.

The House of Lords is the "Upper House" in theory, but has very limited powers. It is composed of judges, archbishops, some bishops, and, previously, members of the English and Scottish hereditary nobility (lords). Most of these have now been excluded and replaced by "life peers" who cannot pass on their title to their children and are selected because they are expert in particular fields or have been of service to the country.

Since 1999 Scotland has also had its own elected Parliament with considerable authority in matters affecting everyday life. Thirty-two Scottish local authorities have responsibility for services such as housing and waste collection.

POLITICS
The Labour Party
Since they took the lead in the trade union movement, Scottish workers have fought passionately for their own welfare. The Labour Party is the party of the left in Britain, and though the distinction between the parties has become

blurred since the era of Tony Blair, Labour is essentially the party whose priority is to improve the lives of ordinary working people. Scottish support was fundamental to the rise of the party—a Scottish mine worker, Kier Hardy, became the first Labour member of the House of Commons in 1892. In 1924 the first Labour prime minister of the United Kingdom was another Scot, Ramsay MacDonald, the illegitimate son of a household servant.

Since then the Conservative and Labour parties have shared power at Westminster in turn, until Scotland lost all faith in the Conservatives after the 1970s. In the 1997 election Scotland returned fifty-six Labour MPs and no Conservatives. In the new millennium, however, the Labour Party in Scotland has been confronted by a major new force: a party committed to complete independence from England.

The Floor of the House
When Kier Hardy was first elected, he arrived in his cloth cap and workingman's clothes. A policeman mistook him for one of the builders and asked him: "Are you here to work on the roof?" "No," the new MP replied. "I'm working on the floor [of the House]."

The Scottish National Party
As Scotland's prosperity declined its people became increasingly dissatisfied with government from Westminster, a feeling exacerbated by the perception that the new oil revenues were being used to benefit London more than Edinburgh. In the 1970s the Scottish National Party campaigned with the slogan "It's Scotland's oil," and by the end of the decade the SNP had gained 30 percent of the Scottish vote and had eleven MPs sitting at Westminster.

When Labour came to power in 1997, it fulfilled its electoral promise to reestablish a Scottish Parliament that would govern the country in domestic matters. Elections for the Parliament were held in May 1999—Labour won the most seats, with the Scottish Nationalists coming second. Since 1999 the Nationalists have built up their support. Following the third

Scottish parliamentary election in May 2007, no party won an overall majority, but the SNP gained the most seats (forty-seven). It was able to form a minority government, though it had only won by the narrowest of margins. The Scottish Labour Party held forty-six seats, the Scottish Conservative and Unionist Party seventeen, the Scottish Liberal Democrats sixteen, and the Scottish Green Party two.

The new government boasted that its citizens were better provided for than the English: schoolchildren had smaller classes and free meals, and university education was free. The Scottish health service, being better funded, had new hospitals and shorter waiting lists; elderly folk got free residential care, whereas English pensioners often sold their homes to pay for their care.

Then came the international banking crisis of 2009. It was to have a drastic effect, and the Scottish economy, so dependent on financial services, had to be shored up by the British government.

The recession demonstrated how much the success of the Scottish Parliament's policies was based on subsidy from England. So, there are no signs of impending independence at the moment—but the situation could change.

THE SCOTTISH ECONOMY
Scottish Gross Domestic Product
Between 2000 and 2006, Scotland's GDP grew by 12.2 percent even though the level of export sales in manufactured goods fell by nearly 30 percent, consequent to the decline in the electrical and instrument-engineering sector.

The Service Sector
The apparently healthy growth in the economy was predominantly due to the rapid expansion of the service sector, in particular financial services, which accounts for 72 percent of GDP and employs 1.96 million people. This overdependence on financial services of course made the Scottish economy particularly vulnerable in the recession.

The near collapse of HBOS—the holding company for the Bank of Scotland and Halifax— caused particular concern because HBOS is responsible for over half of all Scottish corporate lending. HBOS was rescued

by Lloyds TSB, which shifted the focus away from Edinburgh to London.

The other mainstay of the service sector is tourism, which remained reasonably resilient, putting about £4.2 billion into the Scottish economy annually and supporting around 218,000 jobs, or over 9 percent of all employment.

Manufacture

Production accounts for 19 percent of GDP. Electrical and instrument manufacture remain significant but food and drink is the largest employer, providing a quarter of manufacturing exports, employing 122,000 people, and generating £7.5 billion in sales. Other products are wood pulp, chemicals, and still some iron and steel and other metals. The textile industry is important on the borders, with some specialist textile manufacturing on various islands (Harris Tweed, for instance). Tartan cloth alone contributes £350 million per annum, over 0.5 percent of GDP.

Agriculture, Fishing, and Forestry
This sector contributes less than 2 percent to
GDP but has a significance beyond mere statistics.
The vast majority of land in Scotland is under
agricultural use, and the sector is responsible for
much of Scotland's food exports. It is heavily
subsidized by the European Union. In 2008,
95 percent of producers (20,200 businesses)
received a total of £427 million. Forestry plays
a major role in the economy of Highland areas;
fishing is still the lifeblood of many small
communities and sustains tens of thousands
of jobs, though currently it is severely restricted
by the EU quota system.

Life Sciences and Education
Scotland has always been at the forefront of
medical discoveries and today it is a major center
for the life sciences industry, with more than 600
life sciences organizations employing over 30,500
staff and an annual growth rate of 7 to 8 percent.
Scotland is also an "exporter of education," the
number of overseas students applying to study at
Scottish universities having risen impressively in
the twenty-first century so that now higher
education institutions account for 9 percent of
Scotland's service sector exports.

Scotland's Energy Industries
In 1965, oil was found in the North Sea in small
quantities. In the late 1960s and the 1970s, vastly
larger deposits were discovered, including the
nearly 3-billion-barrel Forties Field and the
2.5-billion-barrel Brent Field. Production peaked

in 1998 and has been declining since at 11 percent or so a year; however, in 2008 there were estimated to be over 30 billion barrels left, enough to last for another thirty or forty years. New technology has made possible drilling in ever-deeper water and in the stormy North Atlantic.

Scotland's share of UK oil and gas, power generation, and renewable energy is around £9 billion per annum, and the long-term aim is to offset the projected decline in offshore oil and gas with growth in new sectors, especially the thriving Scottish renewable energy industry.

Footnote for Scottish Nationalists

In 2005 a document emerged under the Freedom of Information Act that has been seized on by the SNP. Written by the Scottish economist Professor Gavin McCrone, and only nineteen pages long, it was sent to the Cabinet Office in April 1975. The professor argued that North Sea oil could have made an independent Scotland as "prosperous as Switzerland," with "embarrassingly" large tax surpluses and the hardest currency in Europe. The document was rapidly classified as top secret and buried for thirty years.

chapter two

VALUES &
ATTITUDES

PROPER PRIDE
The French once had a saying:
"*Fier comme un eccossais,*"
meaning "Proud as a Scotsman."
There's plenty to be proud of,
and not just the scenery and
history; Scottish inventions have
made the world a better place, and
Scottish businessmen, colonizers, and
culture have spread worldwide. Scottish pride and
self-worth still burn as fiercely as ever.

Foreigners sometimes call the United Kingdom
"England," lumping all its people together as
"English." This is not well received in Scotland.
At its heart Scottishness is a pride in a unique
identity, distinct not just from the English, but
from everyone else as well.

Two-thirds of Scots questioned in recent
surveys saw themselves as exclusively Scottish or
more Scottish than British. That is not to say that
they favor total independence; it simply suggests
that they want to be seen as a nation distinct from
England. The huge numbers who voted for the
reestablishment of a Scottish Parliament in 1999
show what Professor Tom Devine has called a
Scotland "more secure in its own sense of itself

than for many decades." Far fewer are prepared to vote for complete independence.

EGALITARIANISM

Scottish self-respect is matched by a lack of respect for those who set themselves up as "our betters," an egalitarianism expressed in the Robert Burns poem usually known as *A Man's a Man for A' That*. Set to music, it was sung at the opening of the Scottish Parliament in 1999. The spelling is changed from the Scottish style to the English to make it easier to understand, but the words are the same. Burns was writing at the time of the Clearances, when few ordinary Scotsmen had any reason to "love a lord," either English or Scottish.

> *Ye see yon birkie [show-off] called a lord,*
> *Who struts, and stares, and all that?*
> *Though hundreds worship at his word,*
> *He's but a cuif [fool] for all that.*
> *For all that, and all that,*
> *His ribbon, star, and all that,*
> *The man of independent mind,*
> *He looks and laughs at all that.*

Many of Scotland's greatest figures were "men of independent mind" who sprang from the ordinary people.

THE SCOTS AND THE ENGLISH

The history of Scotland is largely a record of resistance to English domination, and there is still a residue of bitter resentment among diehard nationalists. In general, however, the Scots and the English are like squabbling siblings who come together when the family is threatened. The apparent antipathy of the Scots toward the English generally owes as much to the Scottish sense of humor as to any real animosity. In the recession of 2009, most Scottish businessmen recognized London as the financial power base without which the Scottish economy would collapse.

One such businessman, however, commented that English reserve and "good manners" sometimes made him and his colleagues feel uncomfortable. Scots, he said, are always pushing the social boundaries and are offended when the English appear to be distancing themselves, apparently almost looking down on their Scottish colleagues.

OPENNESS AND READINESS TO TAKE OFFENSE

In contrast to this English reserve, the Scots see themselves as friendly, down-to-earth, and open. They say what they mean and they mean what they say. On the other hand, a somewhat disconcerting aspect of Scottish openness is the pride a few take in "straight talking"—making their point without, as they see it, being hypocritically polite. To the unprepared, such bluntness may seem downright rude.

Be warned that these same forthright people can be very touchy, and extremely easily offended if you speak to them in the same vein. A Scotsman, an American once remarked, has "a very good conceit of himself" and is "quick to resent any rebuke or even the mildest criticism." The national symbol is a thistle, and the motto that goes with it, "*Nemo me impune lacessit*," can be translated in the Scots idiom as "Dinna mess with me, pal."

CALVINISM AND THE WORK ETHIC
Calvinism is traditionally identified with the "work ethic": hard work creates financial profit, and the gaining of wealth is evidence of being in a state of grace with the Almighty. So, profitability and Presbyterianism march together—making money requires toil and commitment, but it is Godly work. A residual effect of the association of Calvinism and capitalism is financial scrupulousness—if God is to bless your endeavors, He will not countenance dishonesty!

COMPETITIVENESS

A consequence of this "will to succeed" is a marked competitiveness. Bill Shankly, the famous football manager, was born into a tough Ayrshire mining community, and one of his remarks exemplifies the thinking of many Scots: "If you are first you are first. If you are second you are nothing." This attitude runs through a surprising variety of aspects of Scottish life—even "Scottish dancing" is a competitive rather than a group activity.

People in business can be highly competitive too, and like to think of themselves as tough bargainers. As elsewhere, however, this self-image does not always represent the true picture.

Other aspects of the Scottish character can mean that in practice honesty and fairness are valued above getting a cheap deal, while concern as to whether the relationship of potential business partners will be likely to engender an atmosphere of mutual trust and benefit is important to the sociable, codependent, "clannish" side of the Scots.

LOYALTY AND CLANNISHNESS

This combination of mutual trust and dependence, joined with group-based competitiveness ("Us versus them!"), is rooted in history. The very word "clannishness" has its origin in the Scottish clan system, and to this day the Scots have a strong sense of group identity and loyalty. Whether belonging to a family, a neighborhood, a church, a town or city, the freemasons, or an army regiment, or supporting a football team ("football" refers to soccer rather than American-style football), Scottish people cluster together and will go to great lengths to support and succor each other.

Loyalty is an admirable quality, but with it comes hostility toward rivals. Scottish history is shot through with internecine conflict. Today the cities of Glasgow and Edinburgh have little love for each other, while within Glasgow the supporters of the Celtic and Rangers football teams are equally hostile; at the grassroots level, violent gangs of youths identify with neighborhoods and even individual streets.

There is nothing exclusively Scottish in such identification: if you are a Catholic, a Presbyterian, or a Freemason, or have a name associated with some clan, that particular group will take you to its bosom—and in the same way, if you develop links with a Scottish company you will quite likely find yourself treated more like a family member than a business partner, and expected to be as blindly loyal.

CONTRASTING VALUES

Contention and strongly opposed opinions seem to be built into the framework of Scottish life. Scotland's greatest theologian, John Knox, used a profound knowledge of the Bible and an incandescent faith to overthrow a queen; Scotland's greatest philosopher, David Hume, was an atheist whose investigations into human nature were rooted in a profound appreciation of "reason" in morality and ethics. Today 28 percent of Scots say they have no religion, yet plenty of others are God-fearing to the point of bigotry, whether as Catholics or Protestants—each of whom, incidentally, condemns the other to the eternal torments of Hell.

QUARRELSOMENESS

Scotsmen can indeed be intemperate. They often have very firm opinions and are prepared to defend them forcefully. The writer Neil Munro attributed this quarrelsomeness to geology and meteorology: "I am aye thinking that the Almighty put us in this land of rocks and scalloped coast, cold and hunger. . . just to keep ourselves warm by quarrelling with each other." This perhaps explains why in the fifteenth and sixteenth centuries, *flyting* (meaning quarreling or contention) was an art form in its own right, a competition in which two *makaris* (poets) swapped fierce and highly imaginative verbal abuse.

HOSPITALITY

However much they may argue among themselves, the Scots place great value on being hospitable and kind to strangers or to anyone in trouble. Hospitality is an ancient and noble tradition, and hence the most heinous offense in the Glencoe Massacre was not the massacre itself—clans were always massacring each other—but the abuse of hospitality. The tradition, in fact duty, of hospitality goes back far further: it is rooted in the Gaelic past. On page 160 you will find a Gaelic blessing that gives poetic expression to this ideal.

Still today the majority of Scots normally exhibit great courtesy and generosity toward strangers, and expect the same qualities from those with whom they do business.

THE CALL OF THE HIGHLANDS

The duty of goodwill toward strangers originated in the bleak and lonely Highlands, where anyone who could not find hospitality could easily die of hunger and exposure. It is one of the Highland attitudes and values that have been adopted by Scottish people as a whole.

Highland values and culture have come to mean a great deal to the majority of Scots, irrespective of where they live. Indeed, the trappings of that culture seem to matter all the more to those who don't live in Scotland at all. The whole nation is naturally proud of the Highland scenery, but the Highland folk are also seen as something special.

Rosy Faces and Quiet Eyes

In the Highlands, in the country places,
Where the old plain men have rosy faces,
And the young fair maidens,
quiet eyes.

Robert Louis Stevenson, a Lowlander
who spent much of his life abroad

The typical Scottish man or woman of today may be a busy townie with the usual communications and labor-saving paraphernalia of the twenty-first century, but the simple communal life and the quiet, old-fashioned, religious ways of the tall, relaxed, slow-speaking Highlanders—their music, their Gaelic heritage, and the awe-inspiring beauty and stillness of the Highlands—are idylls profoundly embedded in the Scottish psyche.

One aspect of Highland thinking remains alien to Lowland businesspeople: their attitude toward time. A Highland proverb remarks that "When God made time he made any amount of it." By contrast, for the Lowland businessman time equals money; if you have an appointment with one, make sure you show up in good time—even if he doesn't.

The Islanders

What the Orkney writer David Tinch says of his fellow islanders is largely true of all island people: "Recognised for the warmth of our welcome, yet understandably wary of incomers; inclined to be a bit of a plodder, patient, dogged, easy to provoke, slow to react, Orcadians are complex characters. The more you try to analyse, the deeper you try to diagnose, the less sure you are of what you have found."

GENDER ATTITUDES

With so much dependence on heavy industry— "man's work"—Scotland was comparatively slow to emancipate women. Women were seen primarily as housewives raising children, "tied to the kitchen sink" and generally doing what their husbands said. Today, in the modern economy, life is very different: the majority of women go to work and are much more independent, and over half the workforce is female.

More significantly, and no doubt causing John Knox to turn in his grave, women are increasingly holding senior positions at the heads of governmental, business, and other organizations. These include two former lord provosts of Edinburgh and Glasgow, a moderator of the Church of Scotland (what would Knox make of that?), the chair of the Beattie Institute for Cancer Research, the chief executive of Lloyds Bank in Scotland, and the chair of the Joint Council of Mortgage Lenders.

A lot of women, of course, combine motherhood and work, and it has been suggested, with perhaps some truth, that more than in most countries even the high-powered professional women of Scotland never really lose their womanliness and retain a strong maternal streak.

SCOTS CANNINESS

Notoriously, the people of Scotland are "careful" and "good with money," or "canny." *Webster's Dictionary* defines "canny" as "being careful in determining or acting, prudent, knowing, thrifty, shrewd, skillful, clever, lucky, safe, quiet, sly, dry, said of humor as characteristically Scottish." It is a definition anyone doing business in this country would do well to learn by heart.

In particular, "canniness" involves financial acumen. A "canny" Scot, William Patterson, founded the Bank of England; another, John Law, founded the Bank of France, and yet another, Thomas Sutherland, the Hong Kong and Shanghai Bank.

Pride Before a Fall

There is another side to the Scots' supposed financial wizardry: a recklessness that is the very reverse of the qualities in the *Webster's* definition. William Patterson was responsible for the disastrous Darien Scheme in Panama, which ruined a good proportion of the Scottish aristocracy, and John Law for the "Mississippi Bubble," which ruined a lot of Frenchmen and put France off paper money for nearly a century.

Manic Optimism

Recently, the journalist Allan Massie pointed out that in view of recent events it is perhaps appropriate that Sir Walter Scott's portrait appears on a Scottish £5 note, since his own finances "represented a degree of optimism not far short of manic."

In much the same way, HBOS had to be rescued by Lloyds and Sir Fred Goodwin, CEO of the Royal Bank of Scotland, showed himself a true heir to Patterson and Law with his overoptimistic buying sprees, which resulted in the virtual collapse of the Royal Bank and huge losses to his shareholders. This practical, pragmatic people, with their respect for intellect and cold reason, can also be absurdly romantic and wildly irrational.

THE SCOTSMAN ABROAD

"Rats, lice and Scotsmen: you find them the whole world over" is another French saying, and as long ago as 1099 we hear of Scottish knights on the Crusade that captured Jerusalem. The Scots have always been great travelers and colonizers, and for every Scot in Scotland, there are at least five overseas.

Wanderlust

The Highland Clearances are usually cited as the major cause of emigration, but there are other reasons. Some wanderlust seems to send Scots around the world to seek their fortunes—a sense of adventure born of their Viking blood, or perhaps just bold entrepreneurialism. The British Empire was full of Scotsmen; the English ruled the globe, it was said, but the Scots ran it. At least 50 percent of the employees of the East India Company were Scottish, and Scottish merchants such as William Jardine and James Matheson created Hong Kong.

Scots also played a part in the darker side of Empire. In 1770, on the slave island of Jamaica, at least a quarter of the white population were Scots, while Jardine Matheson's early profits were based on the opium trade.

It was as colonizers that most Scots made their mark. According to the 2001 census of Canada, the number of Canadians claiming Scottish descent is 4.16 million, or 14 percent of the population; 4.8 million Americans reported Scottish ancestry in the 2000 census, and in the 2006 Australian census 1.5 million registered Scottish ancestry. Of these, 130,000 were actually born in Scotland, for emigration continued into the 1950s and 1960s.

Home Thoughts from Abroad

Not one of these millions of emigrants, it seems, has forgotten their Scottishness. Various cultural activities identify them as a group, but above all, they celebrate Burns and Burns Night.

This deep-rooted identification grows ever stronger with time: Canada's Tartan Day is a product of the twenty-first century; in 2004 the idea spread to the United States, which now has its own Tartan Day. Even Scotland was caught up and started its own Tartan Day in 2009, while the ever-vigilant Scottish Tourist Board invented "Homecoming 2009" to woo the nation's errant children and their fistfuls of dollars back to the land of their forefathers.

Carnegie and Scottishness

Young Andrew Carnegie and his family emigrated to the USA in 1848. Like so many Scottish emigrants he came from a humble background where "thrift" was a product of poverty—when money is scarce, it must be conserved.

Carnegie's thriftiness and energy enabled him to rise to become, reputedly, the second-richest man in history. His career is an exemplar of Scottish values in action.

Carnegie was "careful" and paid his employees quite low wages, but he was not mean. He devoted the last twenty years of his life to giving away his money, including setting up a generous pension fund for his employees. Having benefited from a free library himself, he established hundreds of libraries, schools, and universities in America, Great Britain, and elsewhere. Except in scale, he is not untypical: the Scots give more to charity per head than any nation in Europe.

A RESPECT FOR EDUCATION

Carnegie was a dogmatic believer in reading and education who put his money where his principles told him he should. Today people in Scotland are generally better educated than the English; they love learning for its own sake, for the way it can benefit humankind, and for the way it can be put to practical use. Higher education is especially valued, a respect expressed with characteristic wry humor in the admiring phrase: "He's got mair degrees than a thermometer." Not surprisingly, Scots universities are world leaders in such practical subjects as medicine, engineering, and technology.

"Touch his head, and he will bargain
and argue with you to the last;
Touch his heart, and he falls upon
your breast."

*Andrew Carnegie on two aspects
of the Scottish character*

THE SCOTTISH ENLIGHTENMENT

In the late eighteenth century the Scots were the most literate people in Europe, with an estimated 75 percent male literacy. England had two half-asleep universities teaching in Latin; Scotland had four go-ahead universities teaching in English and welcoming the clever sons of laborers with open arms and scholarships. This explains how this small, poor country came to lead the world in medicine, technological innovation, and practical philosophy. According to myth, James Watt watched a boiling kettle and immediately understood everything about steam power; in reality, he spent years toiling at Glasgow University, encouraged in his work by the distinguished Scottish scientist Joseph Black, himself the discoverer of latent heat, specific heat, and the properties of carbon dioxide. The intellectual and scientific triumphs of the "Scottish Enlightenment" are central to Scottish self-esteem, sense of worth, and self-respect.

The French Connection

"We look to Scotland for all our ideas of civilization."

Voltaire

Medicine Men

The Hunter brothers, two of ten children born on a poor farm near Glasgow, made Scotland the Mecca for medicine and surgery. Between 1750

and 1850 Oxford and Cambridge produced
500 doctors; Scottish universities produced 10,000.

James Young Simpson introduced chloroform,
the first reliable anesthetic (administered to
Queen Victoria at the birth of her last two
children), and Joseph Lister used carbolic acid
in treating compound fractures, pioneering
antiseptic surgery, which would save millions
of lives.

Geniuses

Among many brilliant minds
breaking the mold of traditional
thought, two stand out. David
Hume was one of the eighteenth
century's greatest
thinkers, his
philosophy directly
influencing the US
Constitution and leading
indirectly to modern sociology
and psychology. Adam Smith is
an even more towering figure.
Smith's *Inquiry into the Nature
and Causes of the Wealth of Nations*
(1776) invented economics, the
religion of the twenty-first century.

Inventors

Hume and Smith were men of ideas, but what
of the practical men—the inventors? Scottish
inventiveness was to create much of Britain's
nineteenth-century prosperity. James Watt's

improvements to the steam engine made Victorian Britain possible, with its steam railways, steamships, and steam-driven industry. Telford and Macadam created the modern tarmacadam road. Andrew Meikle, a millwright all his working life, developed a threshing machine that would change the face of agriculture.

In 1786, the year Burns published his first poems, New Lanark Mills became the biggest cotton mill in the world, soon to be helped to success by Patrick Clark's invention of a cotton thread as strong and smooth as silk and a great deal cheaper.

The inventions went on and on: William Murdoch discovered how to use coal gas for street lighting, and in 1823 Charles Macintosh's new waterproof fabric gave the world the "mac."

In 1827 the screw propeller for ships was coinvented by Robert Wilson and the world became smaller, while the Stevensons' newfangled lighthouses made it safer.

James Nasmyth's invention of the steam hammer revolutionized the working of iron, and in 1828 James Neilson's hot-blast furnace transformed iron production in Britain and America, making it possible to smelt iron ore with low-grade anthracite.

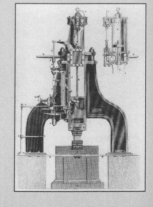

In 1839 Kirkpatrick McMillan, a Dundee

blacksmith, produced the prototype of all bicycles the world over from Amsterdam to Beijing, while John Boyd Dunlop won the gratitude of these cyclists, and of car drivers, for pioneering the pneumatic tire to make travel vastly more comfortable.

In the 1850s Samuel Cunard's iron-hulled steamships destroyed the monopoly of American sail ships on the transatlantic route and started a new industry on Clydeside. So fast was the pace of change that Clyde shipbuilders Barclay Curle developed twelve different types of marine engine within twenty years.

In 1870 the young Alexander Graham Bell emigrated, like so many Scots, to Canada. Six years later, shortly after his twenty-ninth birthday, he patented the telephone, going on to take out a further eighteen patents including one for the earliest form of microphone.

And so on and so on. In the 1930s Alexander Fleming gave the world penicillin and John Logie Baird television, while more recently, in 1996, the Roslyn Institute produced the first cloned mammal, Dolly the sheep. With less than 0.1 percent of the world's population, Scotland produces 1 percent of the world's published research, and Scots—either native Scots or people of Scottish extraction—have won some 11 percent of all Nobel Prizes ever awarded.

chapter three

RELIGION, TRADITIONS, & CUSTOMS

Highland scenery and the Highland culture seem the very essence of Scottishness, but this was not always so. In the late eighteenth century the *General Gazetteer* commented: "The North division of the country is chiefly an assembly of vast dreary mountains." As for the Highland people, they appeared so alien in language and culture that some Lowlanders did not consider them Scottish at all, dismissing them as "Irish." The Highlanders, like the Irish, were largely Roman Catholic, and to all good Calvinists Catholicism was an abomination—the Scarlet Woman; the Great Whore of Babylon.

RELIGION

The Kirk or Church of Scotland is Protestant and Presbyterian. It is independent of the state and the Queen is simply an ordinary member of the Kirk, though represented at its General Assembly by a commissioner. In Presbyterianism each congregation chooses its minister and the church is governed by its members. In so far as such an institution can have a leader this is the moderator of the General Assembly, often wrongly called the moderator of the Church of Scotland.

He or she is chosen annually and keeps order in the Assembly, rules on points of disagreement, and signs documents on the Assembly's behalf. About 12 percent of Scots are active members of the Church of Scotland, with 40 percent claiming affinity to it. Divisions within Presbyterianism in the 1840s led to the secession of the Calvinist Free Church of Scotland. A further break by a minority led to the founding of a stricter Church, today known colloquially as the "Wee Frees." Shrinking congregations caused the Church of Scotland and the Free Church to reunite recently. The small Episcopal Church, which has bishops, is part of the Anglican Communion, and there are also, of course, the Catholics.

Which Foot do You Kick With?
In Scotland, if you ask a man, "Which foot do you kick with?" and his answer is, "The left," he is a Catholic. Roman Catholicism survives in many parts of the Highlands and some of the Western Isles. Curiously, South Uist and Barra are Catholic

enclaves, while Lewis and Harris have thriving congregations belonging to the "Wee Frees."

Catholicism was greatly strengthened by large-scale immigration from Ireland, but not all Irish immigrants were Catholics. Mechanization in the linen industry in the nineteenth century ruined thousands of Northern Irish Protestant weavers, and many migrated to Scotland. Sharing the Presbyterians' hostility to Catholicism, they introduced the Orange Order to Scotland—a brotherhood created to defend Northern Ireland from the Catholic and Republican threat and named after William of Orange.

Religion is a serious and potentially violent issue, especially in Glasgow. Strangely but dangerously, religious affiliations are linked to football: Protestants support Glasgow Rangers and Catholics support Glasgow Celtic.

Green Issues

Green is the color associated with Catholicism, and some Protestants will not allow green objects in their home. In Protestant Larkhall in Lanarkshire, the drugstore chain Moss Pharmacies had to change its green logo to blue, and the sandwich bar chain Subway put up a black sign instead of its usual green one.

Other Faiths

Only 2 percent of Scotland's population is nonwhite and though Islam is the largest non-Christian faith, it numbers only 40,000 souls. In the cities are small

Hindu and Sikh communities, while the Samyé Ling Monastery near Eskdalemuir includes the largest Buddhist temple in Europe.

There is a small Jewish community, mainly in Glasgow: a Jewish businessman who attended a Protestant school there reports that as a Jew he was completely accepted, whereas a Catholic would have been ostracized.

The 2001 census registered 28 percent of the population as having no religion, a high proportion to be actively atheist and possibly a reaction against the bigoted sectarianism of some of their compatriots.

Too Late!
When Al-Qaeda attempted to explode a car bomb at Glasgow Airport, the comedian Billy Connolly's response was: "I love the naivety of Al-Qaeda, for trying to bring religious war to Glasgow. You're four hundred years too late, guys! You've not even got a football team. . ."

THE CLANS
Nowadays Scottish clans are the focus of romance, tradition, and clan gatherings; they play a role in the cultural and social life of Scotland, and that of many Scottish expatriates, but have no other significance. In the past, trackless mountains and isolated glens, each supporting its pocket of population, fostered the separateness of the clans. They encapsulated a way of life in the Gaelic-

speaking Highlands that differed in language, law, and tenancy from that of the Lowlands.

Each clan had its chief, a hereditary piper, and its bard, who in an illiterate society was responsible for preserving the clan's heritage. In Gaelic, *clann* means "family," but although clansmen normally share the name of their chieftain, many clans have "septs" or subgroups with different names. Nor were all clan chiefs Celts—many were Normans, like the Frasers (La Frezeliare) and Sinclairs (St. Clair). Others were Vikings; the Dougalls (Gaelic for "dark") trace their descent from the Norse King Olaf the Black.

Each chieftain had a patriarchal authority and a right of jurisdiction over the clanspeople, who could not hold property—all land was owned by the chief.

THE PLAID

Clans cannot be mentioned without reference to tartans and "the kilt." The plaid, or great kilt, was a

durable blanket worn over a shirt and belted at the waist, with a highly decorative brooch on the shoulder. The tartan patterns, formerly handwoven and colored with vegetable dyes, go back to at least the sixteenth century, probably much further. In battle the plaid was generally discarded as being too clumsy, and the Highlanders fought in their shirts. As there were no pockets, a separate leather *sporran* (Gaelic for "purse") was carried. Some time in the eighteenth century the great kilt was cut in two to produce the modern short kilt or *filibeg*—ironically, among the first to wear this garment in battle were the Highland regiments recruited by the English Hanoverian kings.

MILITARY TRADITIONS

Soon after the 1745 Rebellion these kilted regiments were to distinguish themselves in every corner of the world in the Seven Years War (1756–63). Reputedly the most successful war ever fought by Britain, it led to British control of territories in Canada, India, West Africa, and the West Indies and made Britain the world's greatest colonial power. Later Scottish regiments went on to make their name feared in a series of battles including Waterloo and the slaughter of the First World War, where the young Hitler was impressed by the fighting qualities of these "soldiers in skirts."

These military successes caused a shift in the attitude of the Lowland people to the Highlander and his culture. The Scottish soldier, and especially the Highlander, became a symbol of Scottish nationhood. To this day, for many Edinburgh people the spectacular military tattoo at Edinburgh Castle, rather than the International Arts Festival, is the great summer event.

ROYAL AND ROMANTIC SCOTLAND

Just when the absentee landlords were abandoning their damp castles for cozy London apartments and denuding the Highlands of

clansmen to replace them with sheep, lairds, lochs, castles, clans, and Bonnie Prince Charlie became all the fashion, and the idea of romantic Scotland was born, in all its tartan, pipe-skirling splendor. The inspiration was the works of Sir Walter Scott (1771–1832). Scott was an Edinburgh lawyer who built a house in the border country and first gained fame by researching and publishing the rousing old ballads of border warfare; but his novels, like the early success *Rob Roy*, often retold and glamorized Highland history.

Sir Walter is said to have invented the historical novel; he also largely invented the myth of Scotland as we know it. The ancient disdain of the middle-class Lowlander for the Highlands disappeared almost overnight. Hard-bitten Glasgow industrialists would study to establish links between their surname and an obscure Highland clan, and portly Edinburgh bank managers struggled into kilts and sporrans and slipped the vicious little knives called *skean dhus* into their tartan socks while their wives read Scott's novels, played traditional airs on the piano, and instructed their cooks to prepare haggis.

Highlandism

The wise Scottish historian Tom Devine calls the new Scottish romanticism "Highlandism" and suggests the middle classes in Scotland embraced it because "The rapid modernity made the elites look back for a representation of old Scotland and they found that in the primitive Highlands. . . Highlandism answered the emotional need for a distinctive Scottish identity without in any way compromising the Union."

"Ye Banks and Braes"

The Romantic movement that swept over Europe in the late eighteenth and early nineteenth centuries encouraged a love of nature and the picturesque, and nowhere in Britain is there more nature, or is the scenery more picturesque, than in Scotland. Queen Victoria and her German husband Albert set the fashion: the young couple so enjoyed their walking holiday in Perthshire in 1842 that they returned every year. In 1852 they bought Balmoral House on Deeside and had a castle built there, with all the proper Scottish baronial flourishes.

Inspired by the monarch, Lowlanders and the English started visiting the Highlands in huge numbers; soon Thomas Cook was offering all-inclusive Highland package holidays. That most elusive of tourist attractions, the Loch Ness Monster, appeared on the scene—or rather failed to appear. Canadians and Americans, the sons and daughters of Scots who had fled poverty and unemployment for

a new life in a new world, made the nostalgic pilgrimage back to their parents' homeland. And so it goes on: in 2007 over 45 million visits were made to Scottish tourist attractions.

The Royal Family

The love affair between the British Royal Family and Scotland still rages, as passionate as ever. The Queen's mother was daughter to the Earl and Countess of Strathmore; having spent the best days of her youth at the family seat of Glamis (pronounced "Glarms") Castle, the Queen herself is never happier than when at Balmoral; Prince Charles is frequently seen kilted in the "Royal Stuart" tartan named after the enemies of his House, while the next heir to the throne after Charles, Prince William, attended a Scottish university (Saint Andrews), the first royal prince to do so. By identifying the monarchy with

Scotland, the Royal Family has done much to unite Scotland and England. As to what would happen if Scotland became independent, who can tell? One thing is certain, however: tourists will continue to buy an unlikely variety of tartan goods, and enterprising shopkeepers will cheerfully explain which clan American, Japanese, and Bengali tourists are related to, and which is the appropriate tartan.

The Clan Tartans

Hand-weaving tartan cloth was an immensely skilled, purely Highland craft, but when the Highlands became fashionable the haberdashers Wilson's of Bannockburn spotted a potential market and copied, or frequently created, a multiplicity of tartans that they produced by machine and simply identified by numbers. In 1822 Sir Walter Scott stage-managed a visit to Edinburgh by George IV. His Majesty sported a bizarre version of Highland dress involving pink silk stockings and the once-abhorred kilt in a tartan so gaudy it was almost psychedelic. His statue, in the kilt, still stands in Hanover Street in Edinburgh.

Later, Victoria and Albert opened the floodgates: Albert wore a tartan kilt, as did George, but the royal couple also had tartan carpets, tartan curtains, tartan cushions, and all manner of furnishings in the Balmoral tartan designed by Bonnie Prince Albert himself—which, as it happens, is one of the first genuinely accredited tartans. For although King George's Scottish regiments had kilts in specific designs supplied by Wilson's, notably the green and blue of the Black

Watch (1739), the clans opposing them never did—each clan wore a variety of patterns.

The *Vestiarium Scoticum*

This did not suit the Highland-infatuated middle classes—they wanted the tartan to identify the clan just as a striped jersey identifies a football team. The Highland Society of London (expatriates always being the most patriotic) got a few amenable chieftains to agree that a particular tartan was generally characteristic of their clan, but the game took off in earnest when the Hay Allen brothers, a couple of Welsh fraudsters calling themselves Charles Edward Stuart and John Sobieski Stuart, claimed to have discovered a sixteenth-century manuscript entitled the *Vestiarium Scoticum* that allocated tartans to particular clans. Although Sir Walter himself growled that "distinguishing the clans by their tartans is but a fashion of modern date" and the brothers never managed to produce the original book, the *Vestiarium Scoticum* was to have a colossal influence, triggering the delightful and largely spurious industry of clan-specific tartans—a product not of the glorious Highland tradition, but rather of the entrepreneurialism of the Lowland garment industry. Over the last one hundred and fifty years the system of clan tartans has been embraced and formally adopted by patriots at home and abroad, becoming an emotive keystone in the Scots' sense of identity.

Yet one man, a national hero who never fought a battle, more truly expresses the multitude of contradictions that make up that identity than any checkered cloth.

RABBIE BURNS

Robert Burns (1759–96) was an exciseman prosecuting Scottish smugglers on behalf of the King, George III. Previously he had been a small farmer, which is, understandably, how the Scots prefer to remember him. Like Shakespeare he was no university scholar but rather a man of the middle sort.

To read Burns is to be exposed to all the diverse complexity of the Scottish character—except that he has nothing much to say about religion. Burns could write serious or light love poetry, or about Scottish heroes and heroines such as Wallace, Bruce, or Mary, Queen of Scots; about fairies and fantasies in *Tam O'Shanter*, about his pity for a tiny field mouse, or about the seasons; about love of his country and its scenery, or about a pudding. He could write for and against the Jacobites, about friendship in *Auld Lang's Syne*, or about the daily life of a plowman; and, like Shakespeare, he could take an old tale or song and make it his own.

He sometimes used standard English but preferred to write in dialect. This can be hard for a non-Scot to understand, which possibly endears him all the more to his Scottish readers. The over-reverent Burns industry has put off some cynics, but on the whole people of all social groups identify with what Burns has to say; one middle-aged lady put it simply, "What he said is very true," while a young Edinburgh businessman compared him to Bob Dylan. He is seen as a man of the people who expresses characteristically Scots ideas in down-to-earth dialect.

John Muir, born in Dunbar and the founder of the National Parks system in the USA, summed up Burns's appeal: "On my lonely walks I have often thought how fine it would be to have the company of Burns. And indeed he was always with me, for I had him in my heart. . . Wherever a Scotsman goes, there goes Burns. . . we find him in everything, everywhere."

No Saint

Though Burns is sometimes treated as a sort of patron saint of Scotland, his life was far from saintly: he published his first book of poems to try to raise the cash to emigrate to Jamaica, having got two girls pregnant at the same time.

Burns Suppers

When Burns died, a group of his friends loved him enough to decide to celebrate his life every year on his birthday, January 25. Later the suppers spread nationwide and then abroad, uniting expatriate Scots with the motherland. A fixed ritual emerged. First the meal, with its central dish of haggis. Burns once dashed off a charming bit of light verse about this meat pudding, and this is declaimed to welcome the dish's arrival at table. After the meal the whisky is poured (in Scotland it is spelled without an "e") and the speeches start, opening with the "Immortal Memory," in which an invited guest is asked to give a short speech about Burns. There follows a lighthearted toast to the women in the gathering, who offer the "Lassies' Response" in a suitably sharp-tongued fashion. Finally there are songs, more whisky, and recitations until the evening ends with a cup of strong coffee and the walk home.

HOGMANAY

To Calvinists Christmas is a religious occasion, not a time for feasting. This gives Scotland all the more reason to celebrate Hogmanay, the pagan festival of the New Year.

On the last day of the old year business would be concluded to let the New Year start afresh; houses would also be rigorously cleaned. After the New Year chimes, neighbors would visit each other's houses to wish good fortune for the coming year—and they still do today. Traditionally the first visitor to enter the house in the New Year is known as the "first foot." To bring good fortune, the best first foot is a tall, dark man bringing a symbolic *handsel,* a lump of coal to ensure that the house will be warm and safe, and shortbread or "black bun" so none shall go hungry. The worst first foot would be a redheaded woman.

As the year turns there are good wishes and toasts in whisky. Across the world millions of people, Scottish and non-Scottish alike, link hands and sing Robert Burns's *Auld Lang's Syne*— though few of them know more than the first verse, and even fewer know it to be by Burns.

All's Well

On Hogmanay, among Scottish regiments, the officers waited on the men at dinner; at the bells, the old year was piped out and the barrack gates shut behind it. The sentry then challenged the new escort outside the gates: "Who goes there?" They answered: "The New Year, all's well," and the gates were reopened.

Nobody whatsoever knows where the word "Hogmanay" comes from; it may be Latin, Gaelic, French, or even Greek. The Orcadians, being Scandinavian, call it Yule. Shetlanders, in a determined effort to be even more Scandinavian, have the Up Helly Ya festival twenty-four days after Christmas, when they parade a Viking longboat through the streets and set fire to it.

THE LOCH NESS MONSTER

Loch Ness is one of the duller lochs that run along the Great Glen. It is home to Scotland's most profitable and unlikely tourist asset, a supposedly prehistoric creature that has been identified as a plesiosaur and may or may not exist. The evidence for its existence is a series of "sightings" throughout the last hundred years and a very few, very blurred and dubious photographs. The case against it is that, despite rigorous observation, no one has produced any real pictures, and a number of scientific studies, including thorough sonar surveys of the loch, have drawn a complete blank.

Apologists for the monster explain that she is shy and hides in deep underwater caves.

OTHER MONSTERS AND MARVELS

The Celtic peoples of Ireland and Scotland share their folklore: in Ireland the fairies are never mentioned by name and are called the "good people," while in Scotland they are the "guid folk" or "guid neighbors." The terrifying *baobhan sith* of the Highlands is also the fearsome Irish banshee.

The Norse Shetlands and Orkney are different: in the Scandinavian tradition, they have *trows*, or trolls. The Orcadian poet George Mackay Brown says: "In Scotland, when people congregate, they argue and discuss and reason; in Orkney, they tell stories."

The stories can be about sea *trows* and land *trows*, or tales of the *selkie*-folk. *Selkie* is the Orcadian word for "seal," and the *selkie*-folk are the seal people: shape-shifters who can remove their sealskins to reveal beautiful, sad, humanlike beings. As to how often they can perform this trick, no one seems to know; perhaps at the new moon, perhaps just on Midsummer's Eve. In older folklore they can be very unpleasant, but nowadays they are seen as gentle and melancholy. Anybody who has looked into the great, innocent eyes of a seal knows this must be true.

chapter four

MAKING FRIENDS

FRIENDSHIP AND TRUST

Scottish people have a talent for friendship and loyalty. Trust and honesty are not just highly regarded but taken as the norm. Trust is given freely, and people are expected to return it and be honest and open. As we have seen, visitors can sometimes take this habit of "speaking one's mind" for rudeness, or reply in kind. Be careful; often the very person who is most abrasive will be most offended if you respond in the same vein.

A willingness to listen is a real asset and because family is so central, people appreciate an interest in their children. A wise and rather formidable Scotswoman, when asked by an Englishman what would make her like him, replied: "If you were knowledgeable, showed me respect, were kind. If you were polite, if you were enthusiastic, if you showed an interest in my life." In short, the best way to gain a Scot's friendship is to show sympathy, listen, but above all, be yourself: a human being with a life away from work.

As you get to know people you can almost become "part of the family." This may have implications: friendship for Scots involves mutual support and involvement in each other's lives.

BODY LANGUAGE

The best way to greet a Scotsman is with a warm "It's good to meet you," a firm handshake, and eye contact. Other forms of physical contact, such as hugging, should be avoided—personal space is important, so keep about an arm's length between you. Conversations are normally held in a low, moderate tone of voice; the Scots tend not to use hand gestures, or facial gestures for that matter—at least when sober!

CONVERSATION

In Britain, weather is the standard icebreaker in conversation. Other topics could be travel in Scotland or Europe, vacations, television programs, or golf. Remember, the Scots are proud of their heritage, so avoid derogatory remarks of any kind about Scotland or Scottish culture—the Scots may criticize these things, but don't agree! Keep away from controversial topics such as football, the English, religion, politics, or the collapse of the Scottish banks. If your host brings any of these up, try to avoid offering an opinion.

Bad Language

Don't use bad language unless it is the accepted convention of the company you are with. Clydeside shipbuilders, for instance, were masters of the art of cursing. The comedian Billy Connolly was a shipyard worker and bad language is part of his stock-in-trade, but generally in Scotland, and especially in the countryside and small towns,

cursing is frowned upon. A traditional Scottish
father might not mind his children occasionally
having too much to drink but be intolerant of
even a comparatively mild curse word.

INVITATIONS HOME

If you are invited home for a meal, bring flowers
or high-quality chocolates for the wife and a good
bottle of wine. Dress is likely to be informal—
unless your host owns a castle, in
which case it is best to check! The
Scots make much of children,
so make friends with any
children present. Good
manners and politeness are
appreciated but above all
listen, and show an interest in
family affairs. In England it is
customary to arrive about twenty
minutes after the stated time, but in
Scotland you will be expected to be punctual.

Before or after the meal you may be offered a
glass of whisky. Unless you are specifically offered
ice, do not ask for it—many Scots believe ice
spoils the taste of the whisky. The traditional
Scottish toast is *Shláinte* (pronounced "slancha"),
Gaelic for "Good health."

At a dinner party, the host and hostess will
normally sit at opposite ends of the table, with
male and female guests alternating along the sides.
Wait to be told by the hostess where you are placed.
The Scots eat in the European style, with the fork
in the left hand and the knife in the right (except

for left-handed people), and vegetables and other side dishes are usually served in separate bowls and passed round to allow each guest to serve themselves. When you have finished, place your knife and fork together in the center of the plate.

Politeness matters: stand and help ladies to their seats, do not start to eat before your host, do not criticize the food, and do thank your host afterward.

SEX AND THE SCOTS

Sexual relationships and attitudes to promiscuity are as varied in Scotland as in the USA or Europe. The following are merely statistics—they are not intended as a guide to behavior!

A survey commissioned by the newspaper *Scotland on Sunday* suggests that Internet dating is now a standard way of meeting potential partners: dating Web sites were visited by around a third of those polled. Scots also seem to be becoming more promiscuous: 27 percent said they would be willing to have sex on a first date, as against 17 percent in the 2000 survey. Attitudes to homosexuality have changed drastically: 6 percent found homosexuality intolerable in the recent survey, compared to 20 percent in 2000.

Central Scotland still preserved something of the traditional Scottish sense of moral outrage:

35 percent of those polled—by far the highest percentage anywhere—thought there is far too much sex on television. Surprisingly, Highlanders in the northeast and the supposedly dour Aberdonians appear to be the most promiscuous.

The saddest fact of all: 10 percent reported being frequently too engrossed in television to make love with their partner.

HUMOR

The Scottish sense of humor is subtly sardonic. The English upper classes have traditionally viewed Scotland as a playground, and jokes undermining their pompous arrogance are put into the mouths of the servants who cater to their sport—golf caddies, for instance.

Lords of the Links

A bad-tempered English golfer on his way to a score of 150, blames his caddie: "You must be the worst caddie in the world!" Caddie (dryly): "Och, no. That would be too much of a coincidence, sir."

What is most surprising for such a proud people is that the majority of Scottish jokes are so self-deprecating, satirizing every aspect of Scottish life, including the Scotsman's attitude to women and the weather.

According to Billy Conolly. . .

"Every Scotsman's fantasy is to have two women: one to cook, the other to clean."

"Scotland has two seasons: June and winter."

Don't join in this humorous self-criticism or tell "Scottish jokes" back. Just as the Irish are tired of jokes about Irish stupidity, so the Scots resent jokes about Scottish meanness and drunkenness. Above all, don't put on a fake Scottish accent or call everybody "Jock." Incidentally, if a Scotsman calls you "Jimmy," it's a sign of friendship; "pal" usually signifies disapproval. And remember Scottish sensitivity; don't call anyone a fool, even in jest.

Having said that, and the Scots are nothing if not paradoxical, you may come across another aspect of the Scots sense of humor—a giggling zaniness. One of Billy Connolly's stated ambitions is "to grow old without growing up."

chapter five

THE SCOTS AT HOME

SCOTTISH HOMES

Most Scottish homes resemble those in England—comfortable three-bedroom houses with a decent patch of garden—the main difference being that English houses are usually built of brick and Scottish houses are frequently stone.

Both Edinburgh and Glasgow were noted for their "tenements": apartment blocks with stone outer walls and brick inner walls, typically four stories high, but sometimes up to eight stories. Whereas in Edinburgh these are fashionable, much-sought-after properties, in Glasgow they became slums, many of which have been torn down to be replaced with more hygienic housing.

Castles and Crofts

Scotland has nearly a hundred castles, many quite small and often still lived in by the owners or converted into hotels. The most characteristic Highland or island home, however, is a croft.

Crofts are not buildings; rather, they are small agricultural holdings ranging in size from half a hectare to twenty-five or thirty hectares. The tenant or owner is a "crofter." In 1886, in a belated response to the Highland Clearances, the government gave crofters protection from being driven off their land and the right to pasture their animals on common land. Subsequent legislation has continued to improve their situation; in 1976, for example, tenant crofters won the right to buy their own crofts, even if the landowners do not wish to sell.

Rules and Regulations

A crofter's son once defined a croft as "a small area of land entirely surrounded by regulations," but the regulations are largely for the crofters' benefit.

Government grants help crofters in all sorts of ways, and the Scottish Parliament is working to preserve crofting as a way of life. In practice comparatively few of Scotland's 17,700 crofting families can earn their whole livelihood from the

land, and many find seasonal work in fishing, the tourist industries, or working on the oil rigs.

The Black House

The crofter's home was a "black house" built of thick, unshaped stones and roofed with wood and rough thatch secured with heather. The roof would be low and the windows small to keep out the weather. A central hearth burned peat, and since there was no proper chimney the house filled with smoke and the walls and roof became covered with black soot, which could be scraped off and used as fertilizer. Cows and hens would be at one end, people at the other; little wonder that often there was an illicit still in an outhouse to alleviate the crofters' harsh life. Today many crofts offer bed and breakfast, but never fear—though from the outside modern crofters' houses have a superficial resemblance to these traditional dwellings, inside things have improved.

THE FAMILY

The family is at the heart of life in Scotland. Although families split up and children settle all over the world, extended families, including stepchildren, generally remain close. Family matters take priority, and a family member will fly back from Australia without a thought if there is a crisis. At the core of the family are the children—doted on by parents, aunts, and uncles, and all too often overindulged. A fifth of Scottish children are overweight, and normally frugal people become spendthrifts where children are concerned.

This indulgence does not extend to behavior. Discipline can be strict. The mother is the loving heart of the family but the father is still the authority figure, and a surprising number of Scots report having been afraid of their fathers.

As elsewhere, however, things are changing: a recent survey of Scottish cities found that over 20 percent of young children in the sample were growing up in one-parent families. And because so many mothers work, the vast majority of parents of young children have to use some form of child care, frequently the grandparents.

THE DAILY ROUTINE
Work and Leisure
The Scots see themselves as hardworking—and indeed they are—but leisure matters to them, as docs time spent with the family. Hours worked are much the same as in England. In 2006, the most recent statistics available, the working week was a basic thirty-seven hours (excluding overtime, which had actually fallen from an average of five hours in 1998 to four hours in 2006). Spare time is all too often spent in front of the television, though local public houses and venues such as working men's clubs still exercise a powerful pull on the menfolk, who also flock to football matches on Saturdays. (For a more detailed look at leisure activities, see Chapter 6.)

Meals
Traditionally the three main meals are "breakfast, dinner, and tea," though in towns the midday

meal is now rarely eaten at home and may well be merely soup (broth), a pie, or a sandwich.

Porridge is still the standard breakfast for many people. This might be followed by egg and bacon or smoked fish—kippers or Arbroath smokies. A "full Scottish breakfast" is a sausage meat patty ("Lorne sausage"), black pudding, fried tomato,

fruit pudding, potato scones, bacon, eggs, and finally oatcakes, with that rather unlikely Scottish invention, marmalade, all washed down with endless cups of tea.

The midday meal at weekends may be roast lamb or Aberdeen beef—Highlanders especially have no great liking for pork—with potatoes, root vegetables such as carrots or turnips (neeps), peas (often frozen these days), and cabbage or cauliflower. This will be followed by a "sweet" of some kind—the Scottish people have a notoriously sweet tooth.

Nowadays the main weekday meal is in the evening after work. It can still take the form of an early "high tea" at 5:30 or 6:00 p.m. This may involve soup, a main dish of hot food such as fish and chips, Scotch pie (mutton pie), or smoked haddock, or alternatively cold meats or cold salmon, prawns, or crab. Bread and butter comes with each course and the whole thing is rounded off with a choice of puddings, gingerbread, fruit breads, shortcake, scones, and cakes—with, of course, strong tea served throughout.

Daily Shopping
Towns are served by at least one of the big four UK supermarket chains. Rural people often make a regular weekly or fortnightly trip by car to a large supermarket, which may be a considerable distance from their locality. These trips combine food and household shopping with buying clothes and utilities. Mobile shops used to visit remote areas, but nowadays e-mail and mail order services provide better quality and wider choice.
Street markets in towns are less common than in England, but "farmer's markets" are growing in number. Here shoppers buy direct from the producer things like organic vegetables, free-range meat, cheeses, and seafood caught that morning.

GROWING UP IN SCOTLAND
Respect for Education
In Scotland, most young people grow up healthily within an extended loving family. There is very real commitment to education in such families, with an average of over 93 percent school attendance. Education matters, because it has always been seen as a means to progress—to escape the drudgery that was the lot of so many people.

Glasgow Youth Gangs
Poor living conditions and dysfunctional families in parts of Glasgow have led to high degrees of

truancy and a gang culture with its concomitant rites of passage. In consequence Glasgow has a significantly high level of violent youth crime linked to rivalries between street gangs.

These territorially based street gangs are a distortion of a characteristic Scottish virtue—the Scots are a very social people, and neighborhoods, neighbors, and neighborliness are important aspects of communal life, with mutual support and solidarity the norm.

Underage Drinking

Just as alcohol is a problem for Scotland as a whole, so underage drinking is a problem

amongst Scottish youth. Strangely, the preferred tipple is Buckfast, a fortified wine made in a monastery in Devon at the other end of Britain—90 percent of sales are in Scotland, and on one Glasgow housing estate over half the street litter turned out to be "Buckie" bottles.

Schools and Universities

The Scottish education system differs in several respects from that of England. All three- and four-year-old children get free nursery schooling before primary education begins at the age of five. This lasts for seven years, with classes limited to eighteen pupils—English children have classes numbering up to thirty. Scottish secondary education emphasizes breadth across a range of subjects rather than the specialization normal in England. Most schooling is nondenominational, though there are separate Roman Catholic schools, which are fully funded by the government.

The middle-class public schools (which are actually private) have nothing like the status or appeal they have in England—the boarding pupils are frequently the children of Scots living away from Scotland who want their offspring to have a Scottish upbringing.

The graduating age is sixteen. The majority go on to higher levels, though the government is concerned that over 12 percent of young people between sixteen and nineteen are neither in work nor any kind of training.

Scottish university courses last four years, a year longer than in England—which, it is argued, allows for greater breadth and depth of study. In Scotland, university tuition is free. There is some evidence that this encourages more students from less affluent backgrounds to go to university than in England, where undergraduates pay up to £3,000 a year in fees.

TIME OUT

LEISURE

Evenings and weekends are treasured as time to be
spent with family and friends rather than in
pursuing hobbies. The Scots are a sociable people
and prefer to do things as a group—a group into
which strangers can often find themselves
cheerfully welcomed and all too easily swept along.

This sociability has become diluted, as in so
many other countries, by a universal addiction to

television—99 percent of all
households have videos/DVD
players, and nearly 90 percent
have satellite or cable TV.
Television has not destroyed
reading, though: the Scottish
Household Survey of 2007
found reading to be popular
with 64 percent of the adult
population.

Other favorite pastimes
according to the survey,
though equally "passive," were
those that can be enjoyed collectively: 48 percent
had been to the cinema, 28 percent to the theater,
and 26 percent to a live music event. The favorite
form of physical exercise, involving 22 percent of

the population, was dancing—though more social dancing than the traditional kind.

Sports are taken very seriously, though most Scots would rather watch than take part. Many men and quite a few women attend football matches on a Saturday, where they bond together with their fellow supporters, but over a four-week period fewer than one in five responders to the survey had taken part in any physical exercise other than walking.

A suggested explanation for this lack of interest in taking exercise is that in the past most ordinary Scotsmen were engaged in backbreaking labor on farms, in storm-tossed fishing boats, or in the shipyards, coal mines, and ironworks. They were unlikely to want to indulge in further physical exercise in their brief leisure time. This attitude, it is claimed, has endured into the present.

By contrast, hill walking in the glorious scenery and amateur sports such as rugby were taken up by the desk-bound middle classes and still thrive today. The ancient game of golf retains its huge popularity among such people but is in fact played by all social groups.

Coarse fishing (for any freshwater fish that are not members of the salmon family) is also a comparatively classless activity; however, game fishing, together with shooting, is, at least officially, restricted to those who can pay for it. No figures are available for what the law calls poaching but what numerous Scottish country dwellers regard as their natural right.

All over Scotland and especially in the Highlands and Islands, traditional poetry, folklore, music, and dance thrives, attracting people of all sorts. Recently Scotland has developed its own voice in drama, though theatergoing is another predominantly middle-class activity.

Alcohol has a social role: the pub is a social center where friendships are sealed over a glass and affection expressed in what Burns called "a cup of kindness." Whisky was recently voted one of the "Seven Wonders of Scotland" by the readers of the *Scotsman* newspaper.

FOOD AND DRINK
Treats for the Gourmet and Good Plain Cooking
Most people have heard of haggis and many know Dr. Johnson's sarcastic definition of oats as "A grain, which in England is given to horses, but in Scotland supports the people." Anyone who has tried real oatcakes, herring cooked in oatmeal, or proper porridge with cream knows how delicious this despised cereal can be, but there is more to Scottish cooking than oats and haggis.

Scottish cities have the usual range of international foods: Mexican, Indian, vegetarian, Chinese, Thai, and the universal pizza. Italians have been established in Scotland since the 1900s and Scotland has fine Italian restaurants and ice cream parlors. Thanks to the "Auld Alliance," French cuisine been established for even longer.

The French know something about cooking and soon came to realize that Scottish produce itself can be very special. Nowadays the great French chefs fly Aberdeen Angus beef, venison, scallops, langoustines, lobsters, and that "king of fish" the Atlantic salmon to Paris to grace the tables of their finest restaurants.

All of these taste even better in their homeland, for the essence of the best Scottish cooking lies in the availability of fresh ingredients, which are cooked as simply as possible to preserve the delicacy of their flavor.

Game, of course, is especially good, and venison is quite simply the healthiest of meats: whether farmed or hunted, it is always lean and has less cholesterol than even skinned chicken. Or there is sweet Highland lamb raised on the heather of the hills, or Orkney lamb flavored with the tang of sea grass.

As for fish, salmon can be baked, poached, and smoked, while trout is best grilled fresh from the river but is also delicious smoked. Other smoked fish are Arbroath smokies and the lightly smoked Finnan haddock, which should be poached in butter and milk; some people like it with a couple of poached eggs.

Bread and Sweetmeats
Scottish bread can be disappointing, generally being soft and floury. As an alternative try *bannocks*,

traditional flat oatcakes. Scottish fruit cakes are delicious, such as Dundee cake or the even richer "black bun" served up at New Year. Butter

shortbread tastes wonderfully light and melts in the mouth so smoothly it is easy to forget how fattening it is. Other succulent Scottish sweetmeats are clootie dumplings, apple and bramble crumble, butterscotch candy, raspberry jam, or *cranachan* (oatmeal, double cream, whisky, and raspberries), not one of which will make anyone any slimmer.

Broth and Cheese

Scottish winters mean broths (soups): Scotch broth, made of mutton, winter vegetables, and barley, is world famous, but also try Cullen Skink, a fish soup with an unappealing name but a tremendous flavor, and cock-a-leekie, made from chicken and leeks and the traditional first course at a Burns supper.

Scottish cheese is good, but it's basically English cheese with a stronger flavor. Scottish cheddar remains a firm favorite and makes up 70 to 80 percent of the output; Mull cheddar is to be particularly recommended. Crowdie, a soft cheese called *gruth* in Gaelic, is truly Scots, dating back to the Viking occupation. A particularly good variety coated in toasted oats and black pepper is called *gruth dhu*, or black crowdie.

Eating Out in Edinburgh and Glasgow
Scotland has plenty of restaurants and where you eat is largely a matter of taste (and how much you want to spend), but here are a few in Edinburgh and Glasgow that serve Scottish food. In Edinburgh, The Witchery is dramatically set within an historic building at the very gates of the castle; The Tower, by contrast, is high above the Museum of Scotland. Then there is Rhubarb, out at Prestonfield, which advertises itself as the most opulent restaurant in Scotland but more importantly cooks local produce.

Something Fishy
Fish lovers should certainly try Loch Fyne restaurants, either at their famous and award-winning Oyster Bar by Loch Fyne itself or at their Edinburgh branch, out at Edinburgh's port of Leith. This recommendation is entirely unbiased, owing nothing to the fact that my son is a head chef with the company!

In Glasgow, Cameron's on William Street offers Scottish produce and is very reasonably priced, but closes on Sundays, as is the case with all too many Scottish restaurants. Rab Ha's on Hutcheson Street is well spoken of and a good place to sample haggis; its curious name is the Scottish form of Robert Hall, a nineteenth-century figure known as the "Glasgow Glutton."

TIPPING

Gratuities are part of a waiter or chef's income. In a restaurant it is normal to tip about 10 to15 percent, more if the service has been especially good. The same goes for taxis and room service in hotels. Tipping for bus drivers or tour guides is usually about £3 per person, or £5 for two of you.

Tipping is not expected or even appreciated (Scottish pride!) in public houses, except those with restaurants attached, though it is possible to win a pub landlord's goodwill by offering them a drink—a disguised form of tipping, since they will often thank you and say "I'll have one later." Nor is tipping the norm in hotel bars—however, a tip at the end of a long evening can be a good idea.

Golf caddies expect between £10 and £20 a round; they are poorly paid, and tipping is accepted as being part of their income. Ghillies (see page 129) are highly skilled experts and should be generously tipped if they have given good service—about £15 to £20 for a day at the very least. When out deerstalking, your stalker, a kind of superior ghillie, will expect at least £50.

In addition, fishing ghillies should be tipped for each fish you catch—up to £20 a fish, and of course rather more for stalking ghillies for a kill in deerstalking. If you are going fishing, shooting, or deerstalking, it is always best to check with your host on the local rates for gratuities.

Public Houses
Scottish public houses used to be rather forbidding
places dedicated to the consumption of alcohol,
but many now have a friendly and welcoming
atmosphere with a
range of snacks
and sometimes
lunch and dinner
menus that are
considerably
cheaper than
restaurant food.
They often also
serve tea and coffee

and cater to children, but it is best to ask the owner
or manager before bringing children in.

Smoking
Smoking is legally prohibited in all public venues,
which includes public transportation, public
houses, theaters and cinemas, restaurants, bars,
and offices.

Haggis
Finally, what of Burns's "Great chieftain o' the
puddin'-race," Haggis itself? Well, it is, yes,
oatmeal, mixed with lamb's liver, kidneys, and so
on, suet, onion, and spices, made into a pudding
and traditionally cooked in a sheep's stomach,
though today a synthetic skin is used. It's served
with "neeps and tatties"—mashed turnips and
potato. There is even a vegetarian version, which
may likewise be accompanied by that purely
vegetarian beverage, whisky.

WHISKY: THE WATER OF LIFE
What is Whisky?

Barley is one of the few cereals hardy enough to grow well in the Scottish Highlands. While the French made wine from grapes and distilled it into brandy, Highlanders distilled malted barley.

The barley is soaked, allowed to germinate for eight to twelve days on the "malting floor," then dried, ground, and mixed with hot water; this creates a sweet liquid called wort, to which yeast is added. Having been distilled twice in vast copper "pot stills," the resulting alcohol is matured for ten years or more in oak casks.

By this time it has become a mellow intoxicant called *usquebaugh* ("water of life") in Gaelic and formerly drunk by the poorer clansmen. It is now called malt whisky and is drunk by the gentry.

The Scots say they invented whisky and sent it to Ireland, and the Irish say they invented whiskey, spelled it with an "e," and exported it to Scotland. Be that as it may, *aqua vitae* ("water of life" in Latin) was first referred to in Scotland in 1494. It was a drink of the people and only became a drink for gentlemen in the late nineteenth century, when the phylloxera beetle devastated French vineyards and made brandy scarce. Since then the usual Scots mythology has grown up around whisky, notably around single malts.

Single Malts

Single malts are the aristocrats of whisky, each the unmixed product of one specific distillery. Speyside in northeast Scotland produces over fifty single malts, but single malt distilleries are found all over the Highlands, and there are even a couple in the Lowlands. The other great center for malts is the Isle of Islay (pronounced "aye-la"), where the whiskies have a distinct smoky, peaty taste. This is most marked in Laphroaig (pronounced "laf-roy-ag"), Prince Charles's favorite whisky.

A whisky aficionado will tell you it is permissible to use mixers, soda, or branch water with blended whiskies, but single malts must be drunk neat—and he'll probably have the purple nose to prove this to be his own practice. Speaking of noses, the accepted way to approach a fine whisky is to hold the glass in your cupped hands or by the stem and inhale the aroma. Then sip; don't swallow it in one gulp.

Vatted Malts

Vatted malts are blended from several malt whiskies but never contain any grain whisky (made from a cereal other than barley).

For example, the quaintly named Sheep Dip is, as the makers say, "woven" from sixteen different malts.

"Dinna Droon the Miller"
The miller is the supplier of the barley grain. This plea prohibits adding too much water to the fruits of his labor.

Blended Whiskies
Everyday blended whiskies such as Haig, Grant's, and Johnny Walker are a mixture of malt and cheaper grain spirit, often with as little as 35 percent malt. Most people add water, soda, lemonade, or ginger ale. Whisky,

by the way, is naturally colorless—you'll be told that the color is picked up from the cask, but in practice, coloring in the form of small amounts of spirit caramel has been added since the 1840s.

A Royal Gaff
The late Prince William of Gloucester told how, as honorary colonel of a Highland regiment, he was invited to the officers' mess and committed the dreadful solecism of asking for a gin. There was a frozen silence, and then the bar sergeant coldly informed His Highness that he regretted that they kept no gin, but there was a choice of over a hundred whiskies.

What Not to Do
One final warning—almost everywhere in Scotland, adding Coca-Cola to any Scotch is virtually a hanging offense.

The Downside of Scottish Food and Drink
Despite the fresh, healthy foods available, a recent
government report entitled "Towards a Healthier
Scotland" found that diet is a major cause of poor
health for the Scots. The standard diet is high in
fat, salt, and sugar, and low in fruit and
vegetables—even pizzas are sometimes deep-fried!

The Scots have a reputation for heavy drinking.
Surveys indicate that 50 percent of men and
30 percent of women exceed recommended levels,
and around a thousand people a year die from
alcohol poisoning. The English have no cause to
scoff, however: alcohol consumption throughout
Britain has more than doubled since the 1950s,
notably since the early 1990s against a backdrop
of falling consumption in most of the EU.

SHOPPING FOR PLEASURE
High-Quality Textiles
Obviously, tartans are popular. There are kilts, of
course, but skirts, ties, shawls, and plaids are more
practical, or if you must, tartan hats—the Scots
call them "bonnets"—and teddy bears. You can,
of course, also purchase every item of Scottish
evening dress—not just the kilt, but the dress
jacket, socks, frilly shirt, sporran, and so on.

Better than tartan, though, is genuine Harris
Tweed—male or female clothing tailored from
cloth handwoven on the Isle of Harris. It won't be
cheap, but it will last forever. Make sure to check
for the orb trademark guaranteeing the cloth is
from Harris. Fair Isle knitwear takes various
forms (again, make sure what you buy is the

genuine product of this remote island), and there are plenty of beautiful goods in fine Shetland wool—ideally in the natural, undyed colors of the sheep (see Chapter 7 for more details on these island products).

Food and Drink

Alongside whisky there are various whisky by-products such as whisky fudge or Drambuie. The latter is a whisky-based liqueur claimed rather dubiously to be the favorite tipple of Bonnie Prince Charlie—if so, he must have had a very sweet tooth.

Scots Tradition

Along with tartan teddies, tourist shops sell fake, blunt *skean dhus* and basket-hilted swords miscalled claymores, but more attractive reproduction items are "traditional" jewelry—such as the silver or pewter brooches used to secure plaids—or the shallow, two-handled drinking bowls called *quaichs*. These are made in pewter, wood, or silver, or, most striking of all, silver and wood. In 1589, King James VI gave one to his bride, Anne of Denmark, as a "loving cup" prior to their wedding. The correct pronunciation is "kweix."

Finally, if you have a million dollars or so to spare, there are usually one or two small castles on the market. Be warned, though—these also frequently turn out to be reproductions rather than the real thing.

THE ARTS
Scotland has an impressive breadth of culture, homegrown and traditional but also international, most notably at the world-renowned Edinburgh Festival.

The Edinburgh Festival
The Edinburgh International Festival presents a program of classical music, theater, opera, and dance in six major theaters and concert halls and numerous smaller venues from early August to

early September each year. Simultaneously the "Fringe" festival of drama, music, and comedy is held as a completely open-access festival, its organizing body, the Fringe Society, exercising "no artistic judgments on the work performed." Fringe 2007 featured 31,000 performances of 2,050 shows in 250 venues, making Edinburgh the world's largest single arts event, even before you add in the concurrent jazz, film, and book festivals.

Many famous performers were first discovered on the Fringe, including Peter Cook, Dudley Moore, and Rowan Atkinson ("Mr. Bean"); many thousands more have played to empty venues and deservedly disappeared without trace.

Though they make a lot of money from it, some Edinburgh people regard the festival as an annual English invasion.

In contrast to Edinburgh's internationalism, the majority of the many regional festivals are celebrations of Scottish culture by the Scottish people themselves.

One of the Best Years of My Life...
The four-day Shetland Folk Festival takes place over a long weekend in early April and May. It's a crowded four days, eliciting the following comment from one participant: "This weekend has been one of the best years of my life."

Music

Regional festivals are frequently devoted to music and dancing. Scottish music may be characterized by the plaint of the pipes, but at the Shetland Festival the fiddle, or violin, and the accordion are more common, while the ancient music of the Gael was the harp or unaccompanied voice. "The world will come to an end," goes the old Gaelic saying, "but music and love will endure," and anyone who has heard Gaelic harpists and vocalists can well believe it. Or there's the strange, lilting *puirt-a-beul* or "mouth-music": an oral form of dance music without words believed to have evolved when bagpipes were outlawed after the Jacobite Rising of 1745.

Traditional songs in the Scots dialect abound, notably old ballads about betrayal and murder like "The Bonnie Earl of Moray," some of the most famous having been rewritten by Burns. You may see a *ceilidh* (pronounced "kay-lee") advertised; this was formerly a social gathering that would involve music, storytelling, songs, and perhaps dancing, but nowadays music and dancing, both traditional and modern, predominate.

For those with more classical tastes there are the Scottish Opera and the national orchestras, perhaps performing the work of contemporary Scottish composers such as Peter Maxwell Davies and Iain Hamilton.

Most cities have jazz and rock clubs. Scottish rock bands that have made a name for themselves include the Bay City Rollers and more recently Franz Ferdinand, who won the United Kingdom's top rock award, the Mercury Prize.

Highland Dancing

Scottish dancing is mentioned in the *Chronicle of Walter Bower* (1440) during the marriage of Alexander II, where an intricate war dance and bagpipe music were performed. In reality the competitive solo dancing so popular today dates from the Victorian revival of the Highland games.

At the games, Highland dances were first danced only by men, until in the 1880s Scottish dancing masters invented "national dances" for women. Women are still not supposed to wear the kilt, wearing tartan skirts instead. Nowadays both men and women dance national and Highland dances, and over 95 percent of performers are women.

Bagpipes

The basic bagpipe has been known for millennia, and there was originally nothing Scottish about it. Only in the late sixteenth century did the pipes overtake the harp as the favorite Highland instrument. Dynasties of pipers became attached to clan chiefs, the most famous being the MacCrimmons, pipers to the McLeod chieftains, who developed the classical pipe music or *piobaireachd* (pronounced "piobroch").

Your Morning Call, Ma'am

Queen Victoria, ever the devotee of all things Scottish, appointed a "personal piper to the sovereign" in 1843, with orders to play under her window every weekday at 9:00 a.m. not just when she was at Balmoral but also at Buckingham Palace and Windsor Castle.

Literature

Scotland has a lively and varied literary tradition. Foremost among Scottish writers who helped make the Scots what they are must be Burns, but almost equal in influence was Sir Walter Scott. Scott's books are little read today, unlike Robert Louis Stevenson's *Treasure Island, Kidnapped,* with its Highland/Lowland theme, and the disturbing, iconic *Strange Case of Dr. Jekyll and Mr. Hyde.* J. M. Barrie's darkly fanciful *Peter Pan* is performed every Christmas, and for many years John Buchan's adventures such as *The Thirty-Nine Steps* thrilled the world and became great films. Today Irvine Welsh's *Trainspotting,* the Edinburgh-based detective stories of Ian Rankin, the fantasies of Iain M. Banks, and the charming tales of Alexander McCall Smith reflect different attitudes.

Women writers have come into their own: Muriel Spark, Liz Lochhead, Margaret Oliphant, and many others provide a feminine dimension.

Among a multitude of poets are George Mackay Brown, Douglas Dunn, Edwin Muir, and Britain's new Poet Laureate, Carol Ann Duffy, the first woman to hold the post. It was said of the dialect poet Hugh MacDiarmid that when he died the occasion should have been marked not with two minutes' silence but with "two minutes' pandemonium." Little wonder that in 2004 Edinburgh became the first UNESCO City of Literature.

Theater

Scotland has had its own national theater since 2003; instead of being building-based it is pioneering a commissioning-based model previously untried in any other country. This format reflects the success of existing touring companies, and of the Traverse Theatre in Edinburgh and the Citizens Theatre in Glasgow, in promoting the innovative work of John McGrath, Liz Lochhead, Edwin Morgan, Hector MacMillan, and numerous other Scottish playwrights.

The Visual Arts

Visual art in Scotland begin with swirling, mystical Celtic sculpture and half-abstract illuminated Celtic manuscripts. Scottish architecture stretches from pre-Christian chambered tombs through the Nordic simplicity of Saint Magnus Cathedral at Kirkwall and the strange, crowded Gothic images of Rosslyn Chapel to Georgian Edinburgh and modern buildings such as Hazelwood School, Glasgow, Maggie's Centre, Fife, and Titan Crane Visitors Centre, Clydebank, all winners of the Chicago

Museum of Architecture International Awards for 2008. The national galleries of Scotland, exhibiting works dating from the 1300s to the present day, are five Edinburgh-based galleries, the Weston Link and two partner galleries, one in the north and one in the south. Works on display include Raeburn's portraits, McCulloch and McTaggart's Highland landscapes, Paolozzi's 3-D collages, and a wealth of award-winning contemporary painting and sculpture.

SPORTS
Golf
Pride of place among Scottish sports must go to golf. It was invented in Scotland and first recorded in 1457, when "gowf" was banned by Parliament. The government tried to suppress this terrible time waster and in 1491 decreed that at "no place in the realm there be usit Futeball, Golfe or other unprofitabill sportis." Few today would regard either football or golf as unprofitable! Golf, however, soon became the sport of kings—and queens. Mary, Queen of Scots, is said to have relaxed with a round after successfully having her husband, Lord Darnley, assassinated. Her son, by Darnley, James VI, brought the game to London when he became King of England in 1603, and the rest is history.

The world's oldest extant course, Musselburgh Old Links, is first mentioned in 1672. In those days there were no "greens"—"links" were sandy dunes with short, coarse grass, and the number of holes could vary from five to twenty-five. Only in the nineteenth century did the sport become standardized to eighteen holes.

The Royal and Ancient at Saint Andrews is not really especially ancient—the title was conferred by William IV in 1834. The R&A is, however, the world governing body of the sport, and its Old Course the world's most famous golf course. It is a public course, as are most in Scotland, and like all six courses on the site, it's open to locals and visitors for a modest fee. Simply register the day before. No singles are allowed, you must prove you have a reasonable handicap, and as on most major courses in Scotland dress should be appropriate: no denims, collarless shirts, or sports shoes. Shorts can be worn with knee-length socks, and golf shoes should preferably be soft spikes. The Old Course is so popular that far too many people apply each day and the lucky ones are chosen by ballot.

Should you not be lucky, there are the other five Saint Andrews courses, twenty-one courses around Edinburgh, and three hundred and fifty or so throughout Scotland, many in stunning locations. The Loch Lomond course is American-owned and membership costs the equivalent of US $5,000, while to play on the equally beautiful Isle of Harris links you simply show up and put £5 in the box. As elsewhere in the world, a round of golf is a good way for businesspeople to get together, but be warned: it should not be seen simply as an excuse for an outdoor conference,

and your Scots opponents will expect you take the
golf at least as seriously as the business.

Football

In fact, Scotsmen take all their sports seriously,
and if you are invited to watch a football match
(what would be called a "soccer game"
in the USA) this should be borne in
mind. Of the two "unprofitable
sports" mentioned in 1491, golf
became an international
moneymaker, but football became
virtually a religion—and nowhere more
so than in Scotland.

Life and Death
Another of the sayings of Bill Shankly, the great
Scottish football manager, was: "Some people
think football is a matter of life and death. I can
assure them it is much more serious than that."

Not only is Scottish football almost a religion,
it is in fact closely linked with religion, especially
as far as the two best-known teams are concerned.
Glasgow Celtic (pronounced "sell-tic") is the club
of thousands of third- or fourth-generation Irish
Catholic immigrants in Glasgow and was founded
by an Irish Catholic monk named Brother
Walfrid. Celtic play in green, a color loathed by
extreme Protestants, and their badge is a
shamrock. Glasgow Rangers play in red, white,
and blue and are supported by Glaswegian

Protestants. The uninitiated are advised to avoid discussing football in Glasgow! Apart from these two giants, most cities and towns have a professional team with devoted local supporters.

Rugby Football
Football may be the national game of Scotland, but the *futebal* played in the late Middle Ages, such as "jeddart ball" (where, legend has it, the "ball" was the head of a dead Englishman), was closer to rugby football, leading some enthusiasts to claim that this game named after an English public school is actually Scottish. Rugby differs from soccer in that players run with the ball, engage in scrums, and score points by touchdowns (which are known as "tries")— American football derives from rugby.

Scotland's national rugby team has been a frequent winner of the Six Nations Championship, and the atmosphere at Murrayfield (the Edinburgh home of Scottish rugby) during an England–Scotland tie can be electric. Rugby remains mainly amateur, however; except for major international matches, crowds are small, and Scottish rugby players and enthusiasts are likely to be middle-class.

Shinty
A predominantly Highland game, shinty (*camanachd* in Gaelic) resembles Irish hurling. It arrived from Ireland with Christianity, and Irish hurling and Scottish shinty teams often play each other. At first sight the *camans* resemble hockey sticks, but shinty is closer to lacrosse as you can

carry the ball in your *caman* and swing it from shoulder height. It is a wholly amateur sport.

Other Sports

Most sports can be played or watched in Scotland. Even the supremely English game of cricket has over 200 clubs and 8,000 players, while Andy Murray, the most successful British tennis player for generations—at the time of writing, he is seeded fourth—is a Scotsman.

Winter Sports: Skiing and Curling

Winter sports are centered in the Cairngorms. The main ski resort is Aviemore, with all the usual hotels, restaurants, chalets, skating rinks, beginners' slopes, cinemas, chairlifts, and so on. The season runs from mid-December to early May. Temperatures in midwinter can be very cold, and the best time to ski is quite late in the season in March and early April. Scotland also has its very own winter sport. Curling is not unlike bowls, only instead of balls it uses forty-pound stone discs slid over ice toward a target. Curling, which has been called "chess on ice," is nowadays an official Winter Olympic sport.

Highland Games

Trials of agility and strength were a feature of Highland life from the earliest times, but modern annual gatherings began around 1820 with the revival of Highland culture. In 1848 Queen Victoria herself attended the Braemar Games. The competitions she saw were very much as they are today, with stone- and hammer-throwing (each weighing sixteen or twenty-two pounds), tossing the caber (a tall pine log up to nineteen feet long), the long leap, the tug of war, and a lung-busting run up the local hills. Alongside these events there were piping competitions and dancing the Highland fling, sword dances, and another dance called *seann triubhas*, which means "old trousers" and expresses the kilted Highlanders' disdain for these garments.

Over a hundred "gatherings" are held throughout Scotland, usually in August, but the Braemar Gathering remains the most important and is always held on the first Saturday in September because that was the date that suited Queen Victoria.

Walking and Sightseeing

There is a multitude of romantic ruins and ancient buildings worth visiting, including medieval abbeys such as Kelso, Dryburgh, Melrose, and Jedburgh, and Iona itself. And there are the castles—grim, forbidding strongholds at Hermitage or Borthwick, or the fairy-tale clusters of towers, gables, and turrets of Craigmillar, Dunvegan, haunted Glamis, and Braemar, not to mention Gothic revival fantasies like Inveraray Castle or Balmoral.

For those interested in wildlife, Scotland's nature reserves and forest parks have pine martens, eagles and other birds of prey, red and roe deer, winter geese, red foxes, red squirrels, mountain goats, and many other species. Round the coasts can be seen dolphins, Atlantic salmon, basking sharks, seals, and even whales, as well as colonies of seabirds ranging from guillemots to colorful puffins.

Field Sports: Fishing and Shooting

Scotland has been called an "angler's paradise," and Scottish salmon and trout are justly famous throughout the world. In the south you can cast for salmon on the River Tweed and brown trout in the Ettrick and Teviot. In Aberdeenshire the Dee is one of the best salmon rivers in the world. Permits for trout fishing are quite cheap, and while salmon fishing on the great rivers is expensive, dozens of smaller rivers can give great sport to the salmon angler. The use of bait in freshwater fishing is seriously frowned upon, and it is a statutory offense to fish for trout or salmon with set rods or lines— that is, with a rod placed on a rest. Rod and line fishing must be done with a handheld rod and flies.

The moorland that makes up so much of the Highlands and the Borders is ideal for stalking or shooting. Game birds such as partridge, pheasant, and ptarmigan all have distinct seasons, but the "Glorious 12th" (of August) is the best-known landmark in the shooting season, when Scotland's red grouse become the target. Grouse shooting in Scotland is not cheap, so if your Scottish business associates invite you for a day's shooting, they are likely to be hoping for a return on their investment.

Deerstalking

Stalking the red deer requires a rifle, not a shotgun. No one should consider it unless they can consistently put a group of three shots within a 10-centimeter target at 100 meters. The marksman or woman will have their rifle carried by a stalker and will crawl up to within 100 meters of the target before shooting. Never shoot at a moving or badly positioned deer, or in poor visibility. The season lasts from July 1 to October 20, but in practice starts in early September. Prices generally begin at the equivalent of about US $500 a day, which includes transport within the estate, the services of a ghillie, and often the cleaning of the trophy (the antlers and skull). The deer carcass normally remains the property of the estate and will be sold as venison. On the more exclusive estates the cost of deerstalking can rise to thousands of dollars a week.

Ghillies

"Ghillie" or "gillie" is a dialect term that originally meant a laird's servant but is now used for a highly professional fishing and hunting guide. A qualified ghillie can be an essential aide in any field sport and should be treated with respect and rewarded with a generous tip.

No Respecter of Persons

There are many stories about ghillies, like the one about the old boy who refused to show a London sportsman the respect that the gentleman felt he deserved. "Look here, my good fellow," the man said. "I've been out shooting with the King; I shot at Balmoral Castle." The ghillie replied: "Aye, and you missed that too, nae doot!"

chapter seven

TRAVEL, HEALTH, & SAFETY

In the cities and central Lowlands, travel is much the same as elsewhere in Great Britain. The landscape is crossed by frequent rail services; commuters on the trains mostly ignore each other, listen to iPods, read newspapers, or tap away at their laptops. There are busy roads, motorways (freeways), traffic jams, and parking fines. Northward, all this changes; there are few railways, and roads are delightfully empty, if sometimes narrow and twisting. They are also frequently unfenced, and the hairy Highland cattle and sheep clearly feel they have every right to stand in the middle of the road and contemplate life. The people, by contrast, are friendly, helpful, and curious to know all about you.

GETTING AROUND

By Air

Scotland has four international airports—Glasgow, Glasgow Prestwick, Edinburgh, and Aberdeen—connected to over one hundred and fifty destinations, while Dundee connects with London City Airport. Air services from Glasgow or Inverness (the Highlands' main airport) have made the north and the islands vastly easier to visit, with flights to Campbeltown on the Mull of Kintyre, to Islay and Tree for the Hebrides, Wick for Caithness in the far north of the mainland,

Stornaway and Benbecula for the Isle of Lewis and the Western Isles, Kirkwall for Orkney, Sumburgh for the Shetlands, and most spectacular of all, to Barra on the Isle of Barra, with its beach landing strip washed by the tide twice a day.

By Rail

The densely populated central belt has a comprehensive rail network (Scotrail), but the Highlands are not well served. However, the Caledonian Sleeper leaves London Euston for Fort

William and Inverness every night except
Saturday, with connections from Inverness to Kyle
of Lochalsh, Wick, and Thurso, and from Fort
William to Mallaig, with a steam service in the
summer. The Highland rail routes are famous
for passing through spectacular scenery. Buy rail
tickets at stations or visit www.nationalrail.co.uk.

By Road
Most of Scotland is covered by a good road
system. Travel in the central Lowlands is usually
no problem, except for traffic jams on the access
roads to Edinburgh and Glasgow during morning
and evening rush hours (7:30–9:30 a.m. and
4:00–6:30 p.m.), and the assaults of the Scottish
weather: high winds can sweep the roads and
close bridges, and even in the Lowlands snow
sometimes closes major roads in midwinter.

There are no motorways north of Perth, but
the last twenty years have seen enormous
improvements in the Highland road network,
including a bridge to the Isle of Skye. There are
still a few single-lane roads in the Highlands, and
many on the islands. These have their own rules:
when two cars meet, the car that first reaches a
passing place must pull into or stop opposite the
passing place to allow safe passage. It is illegal to
hold up a following vehicle and not give way.
Passing places must not be used for parking—and
look out for sheep, cattle, and deer!

The scenery and lack of traffic makes driving in
the highlands a pleasure, but it can be hazardous or
frustrating in winter if roads are blocked by bad

weather—the BBC national and local radio stations
provide regular bulletins. You may see meter-high
posts by the roadside—after a heavy snowfall,
these show snowplows where the road lies.

The Automobile Association (AA) has an
excellent route planner service, and satellite
navigation is available everywhere. Petrol (gas)
stations, often open twenty-four hours, are
plentiful in the more populated areas, but in the
remoter districts can be twenty or more miles
apart, so fill up when you have the opportunity.
Petrol is sold by the liter. There are roll-on/roll-off
ferry services to most of the islands: Caledonian
MacBrayne goes to the Western Isles, while
Northlink Ferries and Pentland Ferries go from
Scrabster (near Thurso) and Gills Bay to Orkney
or from Aberdeen to the Shetlands.

Many islanders have strong religious
convictions, so quite often ferry services do
not operate, and petrol stations can be closed,
on Sundays.

RULES OF THE ROAD

Keep Left
In Scotland as in the rest of Great Britain, vehicles drive on the left-hand side of the road.

Driver's License and Insurance
Holders of overseas driver's licenses may drive motor vehicles for up to twelve months in Britain. If you bring your own car from overseas, you must have green-card insurance and carry your car registration documents with you.

Speed Limits
Maximum speed limits on British roads are 70 miles per hour (112 kilometers per hour) on motorways or 60 mph (96 kmph) for cars towing caravans or trailers. The same maximum speeds apply to divided highways. In built-up areas, where indicated, the maximum speed is 30 mph (48 kmph). Otherwise, on two-lane highways the maximum is 60 mph (96 kmph) or 50 mph (80 kmph) for cars towing caravans or trailers. Police cars, often unmarked, patrol regularly, and many roads have speed cameras.

Seat Belts and Child Restraints
Drivers and passengers in both front and rear seats must wear seat belts. Children under twelve who are under 4 feet 5 inches (135

centimeters) must use a child seat appropriate for their weight; as a general guide this applies to children under about nine years of age. Child seats can be ordered when you rent a car.

Drinking and Driving

Driving under the influence of alcohol is taken very seriously in Scotland and heavy penalties are imposed on those found above the legal blood alcohol limit. Currently, the maximum limit is set at 80 milligrams per 100 milliliters of blood. At most this represents two small drinks, but in practice it is safer not to drink alcohol at all if you have to drive, since the blood alcohol limit can be influenced by other factors than the amount of alcohol consumed.

Using Cell Phones while Driving

Using a handheld phone while driving is illegal. Even using hands-free phones can lead to prosecution if it is judged that you are not in proper control of the vehicle.

Car Rental

Car rental is available throughout Scotland, and as elsewhere in the world you must show your international driver's license and international insurance certificate (green card).

Roundabouts (Traffic Circles)

The priority system for traffic approaching roundabouts varies throughout Europe. In

Scotland and Great Britain, you give way to all vehicles coming from your right and always turn left on entering the roundabout.

THE CITIES
Scotland has numerous ancient and historic towns, but only six cities. These are:

Aberdeen
Aberdeen is the oil and gas capital of Europe and one of the most prosperous cities in Britain, with a cosmopolitan population of 211,000 people. It packs in eleven golf courses, twenty-six swimming pools, two ice rinks, Scotland's largest bowling alley, football, rugby, and hockey stadiums, a theater, a music hall, a conference center, museums, and two universities, and you can ski in winter in the nearby Grampian highlands. The granite buildings can be forbidding on a gray winter's day, and the winters are cold, dark, and often wet and windy, or frozen with icy streets. Aberdeenshire can be breathtaking in the long summer days, however, and even in winter there's good nightlife and plenty of things to do.

Dundee
Dundee stands on the Firth of Tay—a "firth" is an estuary. It became renowned for the three Js: jute, jam, and journalism. Jute was spun and woven for use in packaging, jam (in particular, marmalade) is produced at Keiller's factory, and D. C. Thomson prints over 200 million newspapers and magazines a year. Dundee is an hour and a half's

drive from Glasgow and Edinburgh, is easily accessible by road and rail, and has its own small central airport connecting it with the City of London. The population is just under 142,000.

Edinburgh

Strategically sited on the Firth of Forth, Scotland's capital city has a population of 449,000. The medieval Old Town has its famous castle, and the picturesque Royal Mile descends past Saint Giles Cathedral to Holyrood Palace. The Honours (Crown Jewels) of Scotland, the Queen's oldest royal regalia, dating from the fifteenth and sixteenth centuries, are on permanent public display at Edinburgh Castle, as is the Stone of Destiny.

A deep railway cutting and busy station divide the Old City from the broad boulevards and classical porticos of the eighteenth-century New Town. Edinburgh has the national galleries, an ancient university, international sports grounds like Murrayfield, dozens of good restaurants, and Prince's Street for shopping. Though the cost of living is the highest in Scotland, Edinburgh has been voted the best British city to live in several times over the last few years.

Glasgow

Situated on the Atlantic-facing Firth of Clyde at the heart of Scotland's industrial region, Glasgow is Edinburgh's great rival—for although Edinburgh is the capital of Scotland, Glasgow, with about 580,000 inhabitants, is the bigger city and the commercial capital. Yet poverty and poor living conditions still exist, and Glasgow has the lowest life expectancy in Britain and a crime rate that is double that of the rest of Scotland (but still lower than most big American cities).

Glasgow has much to recommend it, however; after London it is Britain's largest retail hub, with internationally famous brands in its shopping centers, while its buzzing lifestyle led students to vote it the "coolest city in the UK." Culturally it offers an ancient university, impressive art galleries, museums, the Citizens Theatre, with its reputation for innovation, and a music scene that in August 2008 led to Glasgow being chosen a UNESCO City of Music. This accolade made Scotland the only country in the world to boast two UNESCO Creative Cities, Edinburgh having gained the title City of Literature in 2004.

Inverness

Inverness (population 51,000) is set on the shores of the Moray Firth, with the River Ness running through its center. As the regional center for the Highlands and Islands, it is the administrative capital of half of Scotland. Inverness's expanding population and success come from a combination of traditional industries, inward investment, and innovative technology. Forestry, engineering, and electronics are important sectors, and the city has become a center for the sustainable housing movement. As for tourism, the region attracts about a million visitors a year as Culloden Moor and Loch Ness (plus monster) are both nearby. Inverness Airport is the air gateway for the Highlands and Islands and handles more than three hundred and thirty flights a day.

Stirling

Situated where the Highlands and Lowlands meet, Stirling, with its ancient castle set on a rock, is associated with both of Scotland's national heroes: William Wallace and Robert the Bruce. In 1800 Stirling had a population of barely 4,000 people. Then, in 1848, the railway arrived and the town began to grow as middle-class businessmen moved there, commuting daily to work in Glasgow. Today both Edinburgh and Glasgow are only forty-five minutes away by road or rail, but the population is still only 86,000,

FURTHER AFIELD
The Lowland Countryside and the Heart of Scotland

Beyond the cities are the rural beauties of southern Perthshire and the Trossachs, and towns like Dunfermline, Scotland's ancient capital, where Robert the Bruce is buried; or you can step back in time in the cobbled streets of little Culross.

Ayrshire, Dumfries, and Galloway in the southwest have wildlife, historic sites, and Rabbie Burns—most famously his cottage in Ayrshire, though he spent much of his adult life in Dumfries and died there. Lowland landscapes are generally gentle, though there are bare hills and bleak moors in the border country, a land full of history with ruined abbeys and grim castles. Northwest of Edinburgh, the region around historic Stirling is often called the Heart of Scotland. Here are the finest golf courses, including Saint Andrews.

The Highlands

Even if you are you not in Scotland long, it is possible to see something of the Highlands. They are within easy reach of Glasgow; Aberdeen is overlooked by the Grampians, and Inverness is effectively the Highland capital. Edinburgh is slightly further, but a day trip is perfectly feasible.

People speak of the "mountains" of Scotland, but by international standards Ben Nevis in the Grampians, at 4,409 feet (1,344 meters), and Ben Macdhui in the Cairngorms, at 4,295 feet (1,309 meters), hardly count as more than biggish hills—and they are the two highest in the British Isles. To their credit, Scottish mountains do look impressively mountainous because, being largely made of granite, they have a satisfyingly craggy appearance, and the weather and cragginess mean hill walkers and climbers should not underestimate them.

The Islands
Despite improvements in travel—in the past they could be cut off for weeks by storms—the Scottish isles can seem like an older, different world.

The Orknies and Shetlands
These islands are so far north that in summer it hardly gets dark; just a brief half-light called the "simmer dim." The Norse influence is evidenced

by Saint Magnus Cathedral at Kirkwall and remains strong. The islands even had their own Scandinavian language, *Norn*, which only died out in the eighteenth century. Their very remoteness was once an asset that kept them safe from raiders, and there are at least three places of antiquarian interest per square mile, including the famous Skara Brae stone houses on Orkney. Many folk on the islands still follow the old ways— farming, fishing, knitting, spinning, and weaving—and when the modern world arrived with a bang and the East Shetland Basin became a major oil-producing site, the local authorities confined the twentieth century to 2,760 acres round a sea loch called Summon Voe.

A hundred miles north of the northernmost point of Scotland, Shetland is proud of its Scandinavian connections—though somewhat disappointingly its Viking festival of Up Helly Ya was invented in 1870, when local youths improvised the name and started the torch-lit procession. The Shetlands have never been as cut off as they seem, as they were a staging point for fishing fleets and ships sailing to Canada. Lerwick, the Shetland capital, is the center of the wool industry, with garments often knitted in the natural colors of the sheep: white, gray, reddish brown, and dark brown. Shetland wool is so fine that it is claimed a knitted garment can be passed through a wedding ring. Fair Isle, halfway between Shetland and Orkney, is also famous for its hand-knitting industry.

The Western Isles

The Outer Hebrides, the true "Western Isles," are Lewis, Harris, North and South Uist, Benbecula, Eriskay, and Barra. They are bastions of the Gaelic language and culture. Stornaway on Lewis is the only settlement that can be called a town. The isles have a thriving fishing industry but are most famous for the *clo mor* or "big cloth" better known as Harris Tweed. The tweeds are made from virgin Scottish wool, handwoven by islanders, and only tweeds carrying the orb-shaped trademark are genuine.

The Inner Hebrides

Skye, Mull, Iona, Coll, Tiree, Islay, and Jura are the main islands of the Inner Hebrides. Though nothing like as remote as the Outer Hebrides, they too have a slower, gentler pace of life than the mainland. Skye is the most familiar, thanks to its association with Bonnie Prince Charlie and its mountains and castles, but despite its attraction to tourists it remains essentially a crofting area with rough grazing for sheep and cattle. Southern Skye has Scotland's Gaelic college, Sabhal Mòr Ostaig.

Mull is much less well-known and even its forbidding fortress of Duart Castle has an air of peace and tranquillity. Nearby are Iona and Staffa, where Fingal's Cave inspired Mendelssohn. Coll and Tiree are notoriously windy but washed by the Gulf Stream and have some of the highest levels of sunshine anywhere in the British Isles; many of the people are Gaelic-speaking. Islay is more populous, and renowned for its malt whiskies. Colonsay, another Gaelic stronghold, has tropical gardens that bear witness to the mild climate. Jura is home to thousands of red deer and a famous whisky. George Orwell wrote *Nineteen Eighty-Four* there.

Finally, Arran in the Firth of Clyde has lost most of its farming and is chiefly a vacation center, but still has an air of tranquil emptiness and is ideal for the hill walker or lover of wildlife taking a short break from the hurly-burly of nearby Glasgow. A bird-watcher might well be

lucky and spot a golden eagle over Arran's
northern heights.

Sunday Observance
Throughout all the Western Isles and in parts of
the Western Highlands, Sunday observance is
taken seriously. Not only do ferries often not run,
but businesses are also closed and it can be
difficult to find a meal or buy petrol. The Lord's
Day in the west is truly a day of rest.

HEALTH AND SAFETY
Scotland is one of the cleanest, most pollution-free
countries in the world. There are no specific health
risks, and water is considered safe everywhere.

Health Costs
Emergency treatment is free to visitors, and the
National Health Service provides free medical
care to all British and EU citizens. Some
countries, such as Australia and New Zealand,
have reciprocal health agreements with Britain,
but charges are made to citizens of other
countries, including Canada, South Africa, and
the USA. Visitors from these places are advised to
take out medical insurance.

Crime and Terrorism
It is generally safe to visit anywhere in Scotland,
though the rougher parts of Glasgow should be
avoided. Pickpockets operate in the main cities, so
take special care of personal belongings and don't
carry more money or credit cards than you need.

At the time of writing there has only been one terrorist incident in Scotland, at Glasgow Airport, and no one was injured other than the terrorists themselves. Security at all British airports has been tightened and restrictions on hand luggage introduced.

EMERGENCY SERVICES
Dial 999 for the Emergency Services. Emergency calls from pay phones are free— just dial 999 and state where you are and which service is required: fire, ambulance, or police. The police also coordinate the coast guard and mountain rescues.

The Highlands and the Weather
Scottish mountains may not be very high, but they can be dangerous; as many as eight people die on Ben Nevis each year. If you go hill walking, let your hosts or hotel know your plans. In fact, wherever you are in the remoter districts, tell people where you are going and when you will arrive. Make sure your cell phone is charged.

If you should be stranded, stay where you are but do not expect a quick rescue. You should be prepared for a long wait, and you'll need to keep warm and dry; cold, wet, and windy weather can quickly lead to hypothermia.

Take Care Driving in the Countryside
Even on the empty northern roads, care is essential. Beware of sudden gusts of wind, of

cattle, sheep, deer, game birds, and even Shetland ponies on the roads, and worst of all, enormous tourist buses lumbering along in the opposite direction and taking up the entire road.

Midges!

In summertime Scotland can be plagued with swarms of midges. Clouds of these tiny insects, which have been compared to a scaled-down version of a locust storm, are especially prevalent in the west, with its high annual rainfall. Only the female midge bites, and only during the breeding season—unfortunately this is in July and August, the main tourist season! Though not dangerous, her bite can leave a mild but irritating rash.

Carry an insect repellent. Smoke is also a good deterrent—to keep midges at bay, Queen Victoria is said to have chain-smoked cigarettes while out walking in Scotland.

A Web site has been developed that predicts the worst-affected places—the forecast is available online at www.midgeforecast.co.uk.

chapter eight

BUSINESS BRIEFING

Because of its dependence on the financial services sector, Scotland was severely affected by the global recession. In some respects, though, Scotland is well-placed to weather the storm—for example, in the proportion of solidly founded family businesses.

The CEO of a Scottish company is referred to as the managing director (MD). He or she will normally exercise considerable control. This is especially true of family-run businesses, where the chair of the board and the managing director might well be the same person. Nowadays, as elsewhere, the biggest Scottish businesses are part of enormous international corporations, but family firms have survived rather better than in other countries. They are a major contributor

to the Scottish economy and directly employ 900,000 people. An Edinburgh University survey found that of the top hundred companies in Scotland, forty-one were family run.

FAMILY TEA CAKES

Tunnock's, founded in 1890, is a fourth-generation cookie-making family firm with a gross revenue of £35 million; it dominates the little town of Uddingston, seven miles southeast of Glasgow. Tunnock's Tea Cakes and Caramel Wafers are such a part of Scotland's heritage that the company has built up enviable world sales among expatriates.

The workforce is largely made up of several generations of local families and the firm is deeply involved in the community, including supporting local charities. The seventy-five-year-old patriarchal managing director, Boyd Tunnock, is chair of the housing association for the elderly in Turnberry, Ayrshire. He and his grandson Colin, age twenty-three and also on the board, both share a birthday with Robert Burns, which may explain the five-figure sum they donated to the new Robert Burns Birthplace Museum. The Tunnock's Caramel Wafer Appreciation Society of Saint Andrews is one of the university's oldest student societies.

MAKING CONTACT

Don't expect to simply show up at a company's offices and be seen. Initial contact in Scotland is made by letter, telephone, or e-mail, and normally a personal assistant will arrange an appointment on behalf of the boss, even if you have just been talking to that boss. Wherever possible, go to the top—see the MD, as anyone else will be likely to have to refer up to the boss anyway.

Business letters are usually quite formal, and although there is an increasing tendency in mailers to address people they don't know by their first names, this can be resented and it is as well to play safe and address the recipient by title, whether it be "Mr." or "Dr." Recently "Ms." has become the accepted form for all women. Most people sign off with "Yours sincerely" or "Kind regards." E-mails by their nature are less formal, and if people know each other they often adopt the American form of "Hi John" or whatever. With the older generation at least, however, it is a good bet to use the formal "Dear Mr./Mrs." with the person's surname.

Business Hours

Business hours are normally 9:00 a.m. to 5:30 p.m. Monday to Friday, with an hour taken at lunch. Plenty of businesspeople work late, but don't count on it. Make appointments during business hours. August is the month when people with children go on vacation, and businesses are rarely working at full steam.

MEETINGS

Always arrive on time—Scottish business culture does not appreciate late arrivals for meetings or social gatherings. Initial meetings are generally formal and impersonal at first. It is usual to shake hands when you meet, followed by an exchange of business cards, and on leaving it is also customary to shake hands. When shaking hands, give a single, firm clasp and keep eye contact. The Scots like to keep their personal space and do not welcome hugs or other effusive greetings.

Use last names initially, with appropriate courtesy titles such as "Mr." or "Mrs." or academic or professional titles such as "Professor" or "Colonel." "Dr." is only used for people with a medical degree. If someone has been knighted address them as "Sir" or "Dame," with their first name (Sir Sean Connery would be "Sir Sean," and Dame Judy Dench would be "Dame Judy").

After introductions, Scottish businesspeople may well relax, loosen up, and move quickly to first names. They tend to dislike formality in personal relations and can find "stuffiness" a fault in their English counterparts. The human factor carries a lot of weight and the impression you make as a person may well be the hook to judge or reject you. You need to create trust, so if possible find a common interest. Remember that discussing each other's family and children can be a very valuable icebreaker and, failing that, the weather is the common topic of conversation throughout the British Isles.

Dress is comparatively conservative—a smart business suit with a tie is the norm for men, while women should wear business suits, which can include either a skirt or trousers.

PRESENTATION AND NEGOTIATING STYLE

Be on time. Have an agenda, but keep it simple
and flexible—set realistic deadlines and
demonstrate that you can meet them. Don't try
to impress by promising something you cannot
achieve; you're not fooling anybody. From a
Scotsman, "No bad" (meaning "Not bad") is
high praise, so don't blow your own trumpet
too much—boasting, however justified, is not
appreciated in a self-deprecating society.

Above all, do your homework. Scottish
businesspeople see themselves as having a culture
of rigor and perfectionism, and they will expect
the same qualities from you. Be sure that you are
thoroughly familiar with your material and have
mastered all the details, but be honest—if you
don't know the answer, don't pretend you do.

Honesty will be respected. A good
businessman, it is felt, is naturally honest; only the
incompetent or inadequate need to lie. Evidence
of any apparent deceit, including not admitting to
problems that may exist, can lead to a rapid
conclusion of relations.

The Scots have a wonderful dialect expression:
"Facts are chiels that winna ding," meaning that
facts are rock solid and cannot be knocked over.
The practical, hardheaded side of the Scottish
nature respects and demands factual evidence,
so charts and statistics are valuable assets.

The Scots also respect knowledge. Initially
address your remarks to whoever is chairing the
meeting, but watch carefully—you may observe
that there are people present to whom the
chair defers on account of their expertise, and

these may be the people you need to convince. Similarly, in family firms the *paterfamilias* may retain the chairmanship but one of his sons, or even daughters, may be the real power because they are recognized as being more knowledgeable about the facts of modern life.

Avoid jargon and "business speak"—pompous words do not impress. By all means make a formal presentation with all the technological wizardry at your command, but make sure it sticks to the facts. Break it up to allow comment and discussion on individual points—try to bring in everybody at this stage. Make sure there is plenty of time after the presentation for further informal discussion, a chance to "talk it through" and "get to know each other." The meeting may, in consequence, become more open and apparently informal. Be careful, remain on your guard, and stay professional. Your Scottish counterparts will be judging you, asking themselves: could they work with you? Can they trust you? In general, listen, be ready to bargain, and come prepared to give a little ground—the Scots like to feel they are tough negotiators. Be flexible, and above all show empathy and avoid grandiosity or boasting.

Forthrightness

You may well come across those old-fashioned Scottish businessmen for whom straightforward "no nonsense" language is seen as a form of honesty. Don't be put off—there is nothing personal in their brashness!

Various Scots expressions reflect this attitude:

"Are you real?"—Do you have any idea what you are talking about?

"Am ah right, am ah wrong?"—Am I right or am I wrong—with the firm assumption that the speaker considers himself right!

"Yer away in a dwalm."—You are living in a daydream.

East is East

The new Scottish government was anxious to woo Japanese investment—but encountered a real problem. The Japanese business style was polite, ambiguous, subtle, and stubborn. The Scottish style was flexible but appeared stubborn, and was straightforward and forthright to an extent that seemed embarrassingly ill-mannered to the Japanese. The two sides found each other's approach as incomprehensible as it was frustrating.

THE CONTRACT

It is common practice to agree to terms in principle at a meeting, but to review and adjust the details at a later date before signing a contract. Trust is felt to be what matters—"My word is my bond"—a successful outcome being sealed with a handshake and sometimes with a "dram"—a glass of whisky or "liquid handshake." Be careful not to betray this trust by going back on what you have verbally committed yourself to.

All of which is very fine and honorable, but make sure you get the opposite party to confirm the main points of what was agreed on paper or a laptop. Do this at the end of the meeting. Then, as soon as possible afterward and before any papers are signed, send a summary to the other party requesting comments and confirmation.

Scottish law differs in some ways from English law and though this rarely affects business, it would be sensible to be represented by a Scottish lawyer in any legal transactions.

CONFLICT RESOLUTION
If disagreement arises, it should be handled carefully—even hard-boiled businessmen can be easily offended. Try to be completely straightforward about issues without actually saying someone is wrong; it can be a good idea to admit your own mistakes, but don't overdo it. Rather than suggest the other party is in error, say that "We have a bit of a problem." Never question your counterpart's integrity. Don't try to pass the buck by blaming someone not present; this can produce the response, "If he says that about him behind his back, what will he say about me?" Make an effort to conduct the discussion in a quiet, moderate tone of voice. At the end, do not promise to do something and then fail to do it.

As long as you can avoid giving offense or rousing the rage that lies dormant in a good number of Scots, they can be very reasonable and flexible; honest disagreements can usually be resolved, and can sometimes even strengthen the bond between the parties. Nevertheless, don't go alone to the conflict resolution meeting, and take notes, without doing so too ostentatiously. A witness and notes will be needed if you have to make use of Scotland's excellent civil law system.

BUSINESS ENTERTAINMENT

Breakfast meetings are not the Scots style: lunch and dinner are usually the preferred times for business entertainment. Most likely you will be invited not to lunch, but for "dinner." This will frequently take the form of a formal evening meal at your counterpart's home, together with their spouse and even family. In all likelihood your hosts will ask their family what they thought of you after you leave.

Trial by Lunch
The very successful director of an insurance company would always arrange an 11:30 a.m. meeting, continuing through lunch. By the end he would have a pretty shrewd idea of whether he wanted to go forward. Not that he would give you business just because he liked you—but it would be an important start.

At the end of a restaurant meal the other party will probably offer to pay, but even if they are officially the host, offer to pay the bill yourself. Surprisingly often the offer will be accepted—even the most generous will see this as a small victory in keeping with his self-image as a canny Scot, and warm toward you all the more. Ladies, however, are rarely expected to pay.

Gift Giving
Business gifts can be the usual desk accessories
with your company logo, such as a paperweight or
pen set. Other suitable presents would be a coffee-
table book about your country or city, or perhaps a
single malt whisky. Tastes in whisky differ, but you
should be safe with a Glenfiddich, a Glenmorangie,
or a Glenlivet.

WOMEN IN BUSINESS
It cannot be denied that Scotland still has a long way
to go toward genuine equality (though officially,
equal rights are guaranteed by law). Having said that,
women in Scotland have the best chance in Britain of
reaching the top. The Grant Thornton International
Business Survey covered thousands of women in
scores of countries. It showed Scottish companies
had the highest proportion of female senior
managers in Great Britain: 21 percent, which is
2 percent more than London and 9 percent more
than eastern England.

Gone are the days when any woman in a business
meeting was assumed to be a secretary, but Scotland
remains a somewhat traditionalist country:
gentlemen are expected to behave toward ladies
with old-fashioned good manners, and
businesswomen are expected to dress conservatively.
Otherwise women can impress in the same way
as men—by displaying a thorough knowledge
of their field, maintaining a
professional demeanor, and
generally giving the impression
of competence.

chapter nine

COMMUNICATION

LANGUAGE

Lallans (meaning "Lowlands") is a specifically Scottish form of English. Burns wrote:

They took nae [no] pains their speech to balance,
Or rules to gie [give];
But spak [spoke] their thoughts in plain, braid
[broad] lallans,
Like you or me.

Burns was talking about his native dialect and, spelling apart, that particular verse is in pretty straightforward English. More recently, "Lallans" has come to denote a patriotic literary form that never uses an English word when an obscure Scottish one is available. It is spelled phonetically in a way that reflects not just the Scottish accent but the spelling and usage of the time before England and Scotland were linked.

What Burns spoke can more accurately be designated as "broad" Scots, and you will probably hear it spoken. It contains dialect words and forms derived from what used to be called "Inglis": the Northumbrian Angles' version of Old English. In practice a strong accent, especially that of Glasgow, is likely to be more confusing than the use of dialect. Foreigners who have learned English at school, and even many English speakers, can have difficulty understanding what is being said, but constantly asking people to repeat themselves can cause offense.

Some basic dialect words you may come across: *Aye*: yes; *bairn*: child; *bevy*: an alcoholic drink; *brae*: a hillside; *ceilidh*: a dance; *crabit*: irritable, crabby; *dour*: grim, gloomy; *fair*: moderately; *glen*: a narrow and deep mountain valley; *ken*: know, understand; *nay, nae*, or *nar*: no or not; *neeps*: turnips; *tattie*: potato; *wee*: small; *wheesht*: be quiet.

There is also a tendency to end words in "-ie". *Wifie*: wife or woman; *laddie*: lad or boy; *bonnie*: beautiful (from the French *bon*, meaning "good"); *haddie*: haddock; and of course, *footie*: football.

Highland and Island Accents
Inverness folk are said to speak the purest English in Britain and generally the slow, careful speech of the Highlands and the west is easier to understand than heavy Glaswegian. Its lilting clarity probably derives from that of Gaelic, which pronounces every syllable. The Northern Isles still have hundreds of dialect words derived from Norwegian. The Orkneyman, it has been said, speaks deliberately and is not overly given to speaking at all, believing "a man can't learn much by hearing himself talk."

Gaelic
Gaelic (pronounced "gal-ick" in Scotland, rather than "gay-lick" as in Ireland) is related to Irish. There are about 60,000 fluent Gaelic speakers in modern

Scotland, mostly in the far north and the Hebrides. The biggest concentration, however, is in Glasgow, which has 10,000. The language also survives in Canada: Cape Breton Island has a Gaelic-speaking community and a Gaelic faculty at Saint Francis Xavier University.

Largely because of its wealth of poetry, storytelling, music, and song, Gaelic has an influence on Scottish culture and identity far wider and deeper than the number of actual speakers would suggest. Unlike Welsh and Irish, Gaelic is not an official language, but it has shown greater resilience than Irish Gaelic has in the Irish Republic.

There has actually been a resurgence in Gaelic over the last twenty years, from Gaelic-speaking primary schools to further education college courses taught wholly in Gaelic. Radio nan Gàidheal broadcasts daily throughout Scotland, and there are an increasing number of Gaelic-language television programs.

A Gaelic Blessing

"May the holy sunlight shine on you like a great peat fire, so that stranger and friend may come and warm himself at it. And may light shine out of the two eyes of you, like a candle set in the window of a house, bidding the wanderer come in out of the storm. And may the blessing of the rain be on you, may it beat upon your Spirit and wash it fair and clean, and leave there a shining pool where the blue of Heaven shines, and sometimes a star."

THE MEDIA
Television
The BBC television channels BBC One and
BBC Two broadcast throughout Great Britain,
but in Scotland they take the form of BBC One
and BBC Two Scotland, with news and programs
of specifically Scottish interest, even occasionally
in Gaelic.

The three commercial network
channels (these are funded by
advertisements, whereas the
BBC is funded by TV license
fees) are the Scottish versions of
ITV1 (Independent Television 1),
Channel 4, and Channel 5. There is
also a variety of satellite, digital, and
cable channels. TeleG provides a daily Gaelic
digital TV channel, and a Gaelic BBC
channel, BBC Alba, has just been launched.

Radio
UK-wide the BBC has five radio networks,
plus the BBC World Service and several digital
channels, including an Asian service. Additionally
BBC Radio Scotland and the BBC Gaelic radio
station broadcast specifically Scottish programs,
as do sixteen local and independent radio
stations. The major British commercial stations
can only be received in the more densely
populated areas.

Newspapers
Scotland has three national papers—the
Scotsman, Herald, and *Daily Record*—and over

eighty local newspapers, together with a vast corpus of magazines. The main British papers, including the *Guardian, Financial Times,* and *Independent,* are available throughout Scotland. The *Times, Daily Express, Daily Mirror,* and *Daily Mail* all publish Scottish editions. Leading foreign newspapers are available in the main cities.

NEWSPAPERS ONLINE

www.scotsman.com (*The Scotsman*)

www.dailyrecord.co.uk (*The Daily Record*)

www.theherald.co.uk (*The Herald*)

www.scotsmagazine.com (*The Scots Magazine*)

The Scots Magazine is the most widely read Scottish-interest publication. First published in 1739, it is a monthly periodical with around 300,000 readers worldwide.

Business Addresses
For information on the addresses and telephone numbers of Scottish businesses, consult the Yellow Pages at www.yell.co.uk.

TELEPHONES AND THE INTERNET
Scotland has no separate country code. Britain's country code is 44. In 2007, more households had cell phones than had landlines.

In the last quarter of 2008 it was estimated that 60 percent of Scottish homes had Internet access, but the percentage increases daily.

MAIL

Postage rates vary depending on the size and weight of what is being sent and the rapidity with which you want it delivered. Inquire at a post office or go to the Royal Mail Web site at

www.royalmail.com.

Airmail postage for a standard letter is 50p within Europe and 81p to the rest of the world. Within Britain, first-class (rapid) postage for a letter is 36p and second-class (normal) is 27p. Registered mail, with proof of delivery, is £1.08.

Post Offices

The mail service in even the remotest areas of Scotland is generally good, and rural Scotland has been spared the severe reduction in post offices suffered by the rest of Britain. In many hamlets the combined post office and local shop is an important focal point and social center.

CONCLUSION

The small Scottish nation has left a big mark on the planet, and the Scots are well aware of it. Proud and easily hurt, kindly and bellicose, prudent businessmen and wild gamblers, producing some of the best food in the world and eating some of the worst, bigoted and free-spirited, tightfisted and generous-hearted—the Scots are nothing if not contrary.

If you show a real interest in their lives, if you are honest and "your own man" (or woman), and if you respect their sensitivities, you will find them as "affable to strangers" as they were to the traveler and writer William Lithgow nearly four hundred years ago.

"Now as for the gentry of the kingdom, certainly as they are generous, manly and full of courage, so are they courteous, discreet, learned scholars, well read in the best histories. . . that for a general complete worthiness, I never found their matches amongst the best people of foreign nations; being also good house-keepers, affable to strangers, and full of hospitality."

William Lithgow, *Rare Adventures and Paineful Peregrinations*, 1632

Further Reading

Baxter, Colin. *The Scotland Visitor Guide*. Guilford, Conn.: Globe Pequot Press, 2008.

Devine, Thomas Martin. *The Scottish Nation: A History, 1700–2000*. London: Penguin Books, 2001.

Devine, Thomas Martin, et al. *The Transformation Of Scotland: The Economy Since 1700*. Edinburgh: Edinburgh University Press, 2005.

Herman, Arthur. *How the Scots Invented the Modern World*. New York: Three Rivers Press, 2002.

Hood, Neil, Jeremy Peat, et al. *Scotland in a Global Economy: The 2020 Vision*. New York: Palgrave Macmillan, 2003.

Humphreys, Rob, Colin Hutchison, and Donald Reid. *The Rough Guide to Scotland*. London: Rough Guides, 2006.

Mackie, J. D., et al. *A History of Scotland*. New York: Penguin Group (USA), 1980.

Massie, Allan. *101 Great Scots*. Edinburgh: Chambers, 1987.

Massie, Allan, et al. *Scotland and Free Enterprise*. London: Aims of Industry, 1991.

McCrone, David. *Understanding Scotland: the Sociology of a Nation*. London and New York: Routledge, 2001.

Mitchison, Rosalind. *A History of Scotland*. London and New York: Routledge, 2002.

Prebble, John. *Culloden*. London: Secker & Warburg, 1962.

Prebble, John. *The Highland Clearances*. London: Secker & Warburg, 1963.

Prebble, John. *Glencoe: The Story of the Massacre*. London: Secker & Warburg, 1966.

Simpson, William Douglas. *Portrait of the Highlands*. London: Hale, 1969.

Stidwell, Allen. *Touring Scotland: The Complete Touring Guide*. Basingstoke, Hampshire: Automobile Association, 1987.

Yapp, Peter. *The Travellers' Dictionary of Quotation*. London and New York: Routledge, 1988.

Useful Resources

www.scotland.gov.uk
The Web site of the Scottish government

www.visitscotland.com
Scottish Tourist Board site

www.gaelic-scotland.co.uk
Official Gaelic tourism site

culture smart! **scotland**

Index

culture smart! scotland

Acknowledgments

Many thanks to the following for their help and advice: Alister Tulloch, Stella Macdonald, Wilma Hamilton, Peter McCann, Garry McDougall and friends, Iain McCabe, Elizabeth Harris, and Edward Scotney.